THE

PARENTS

SUZANNE CHIMA

DEDICATION

This book is dedicated to my father, David J. Hatfield February 23, 1943, to June 6, 2012, whom I have never met but searched for in my heart endlessly. I'm sorry that we never got a chance to meet, but just knowing that you existed and that I wasn't nutzo gave me the strength to get off my ass and write this book. I miss you and think of you every day!

And my old friend Gary who tried desperately to guide me even when I was reluctant to listen. You were a great teacher and mentor to me, and I will always be grateful.

To my other many mentors, Dr. Joe Dispenza, Dr. Bruce Lipton, Abraham/Ester Hicks, and so many more, who unknowingly and generously helped me shift my limiting beliefs, expand my mind, and change my life, thank you.

To my three children, Brandon (Bamm), Jared (Snuggs), and Samantha (Mammy), you are my inspiration as I painfully watched you deal with so many unnecessary circumstances that were out of their control. You managed to become amazing human beings. You are so worthy of great things and all life has to offer. I'm so proud of you!

And last but never least, my best friend and fabulous sexy husband Tony Chima, AKA "Cheems," I have never loved an appreciated a man the way I do you. I know now that not all humans are rotten and untrustworthy. You mean the world to me, and your constant support and generosity never go unseen. And the love you have shown me will forever change my life. I love you, thank you! 

TABLE OF CONTENTS

ACKNOWLEDGEMENTS

To my kids.

Brandon, "Bamm," my 1ˢᵗ son, #1, born in June of 1997. You will always have my heart. The memories I have of you as a child and our relationship back then will never leave me. Our cartoon and chocolate chip cookie days are forever burned into my heart. Your smile, big beautiful green eyes, and your genuine love for humanity melt me. You are a kind, generous, and wonderful human being, and I'm so proud of the man you are becoming.

Jared, "Snuggs," 2ⁿᵈ son, born in March of 2001. You are an amazing human being. Always by my side as a baby, holding on with such a grip. You are smart, handsome, and so very independent, yet you always have time for me, and I appreciate that. I am so proud of the man you are becoming. I love our talks and our hugs.

Samantha, "Mammy," my baby girl, born in March of 2001. You are an incredible young woman. Your beauty surpasses any that I've seen or known. You are so loyal and brave. You have taught me so much about being a better human being and about life. Thank you for always having my back and for pushing through all the barriers that were in your way to get to me. Thank you for lending your beautiful face for the cover of this book. I'll never forget your loyalty and strength.

I hope one day you all get a chance to read this and learn the truth about me. There is always another side and more than one perspective in every situation, and this is mine. I love you, and nothing will ever change that!

And to my amazing husband, Cheems, you are a great inspiration to anyone who is lucky enough to be in your energy. I love you and truly thank you for not making my writing books and living my best life anything but a great, easy vibe. Thank you for your patience, your kindness, and especially your unconditional love for my children and for me. You are one of a kind!

INTRODUCTION

After several years of abuse and trauma throughout my childhood and adult life, I finally realized that at the heart of it all, abuse stems back to generations of programming from my parents, their parents, and so on. It is said that this programming could have even begun going back hundreds or maybe thousands of generations. And it keeps repeating for all of us from the moment we are in our mother's womb.

The belief systems affect us all during our development while transitioning from a child into an adult. The repeated patterns and behaviors that are burned into us are adopted from our parent's belief systems, past down from generations, as well as our environment. Abuse, lies, deceit, narcissism, forgiveness, trust, insecurities, low self-esteem, anger, hatred, racism, traditions, religion, marriage, divorce, addiction, character, and so on.

It's like an endless loop that continues to be passed down from the family line until one lucky soul has that lightbulb moment and surrenders to the idea of breaking free or to the notion that something just doesn't feel right. I was that lucky soul.

Here I share my story of overcoming emotional, sexual, and physical abuse, the absence of family and friends, my failed relationships, losing my children to a narcissist, losing my voice, my home and business, financial failure, mental stability, and my perceived identity. Along the way, I also learned to connect and tap into my inner being. That changed my life and everything I thought was real.

My life was a series of repeated patterns, much like hiccups day after day, year to year. I hated my life, and I hated the only options I thought I had. I felt like I was living for everyone else and under the influence of everyone else's weird, sick rules, like a puppet, a walking zombie.

But eventually, forty-five years later, I woke up. To many, it may seem too late for change. But change leading to good is never too late. I want to share my crazy story of how I survived every kind of abuse from my childhood up until my older years and made a complete recovery in every area of my life. It was an arduous journey, for sure. But every effort was worth the peace and prosperity I finally got to experience.

At a very young age, I began to have many transcendental experiences and visions. I would leave my body through astral travel, see, and communicate with spirits, and a lot of times, I would just know very specific things. But this kind of stuff was something no one discussed back then, and I guess neither believed in it. In fact, if you told anyone that you just saw a dead person in your bedroom, they would think you were nuts. I really feel that if someone in my life supported what I was experiencing back then, whether it was spiritual or emotional, I wouldn't have been so disconnected. But in all reality, I know that broken people cannot fix broken people.

I wasted years and years doing what I was taught and trained to do by the people I was forced to be around. I believe now deep in my soul that we've all been programmed subconsciously and hardwired mentally, even on a cellular level, by "The Parents," their parents, and generations before them. I don't know about you, but I'm pretty sure that for most of us, *the last thing we want is to be exactly like our parents.*

This hardwiring comes from our parent's belief system, our DNA, yes, it's even embedded in our genes on a cellular level, and our environmental situation plays a very large part as well. Everyone and everything have the tendency to influence us if we let them, and unfortunately, most of us have little choice when we are children in the developmental stages of our life.

In fact, children do not develop high-level critical thinking skills until around the age of five to nine years old, so they must first make progress along four different tracks: developing basic reasoning skills and interest, building self-esteem, learning emotional management skills, and internalizing social norms that value critical thinking.

For the most part, until we can accomplish these things, we are doomed to soak in information hand-fed to us by our parents and our environment. And most likely, if our parents have low self-esteem, emotional issues, maybe a poverty mindset due to their environment, or they do not know how to or are not encouraged at a young age to have clear expectations and or comprehend specific situations, BOOM! They are clones of their DNA. That DNA is programmed by their parents based on their belief system and environment and passed down to the next generation.

Our friends, teachers, coworkers, and family members play a huge part in the developmental stages of our lives and even moving forward into adulthood. Sometimes I look around and feel like there are generations of walking zombies everywhere who are following the same belief systems that were programmed into them from the time they were children. I sit back in amazement, watching people on auto drive or in default mode. Simply unconscious for 95% of their day, and they have no idea.

I had no idea that I was doing the very same for the first half of my life as well. We are literally in an energy bubble that attaches to other people's energy bubbles around us, doing pretty much the same things day after day, week after week, month after month, and so on. That is unless, of course, we take an interest in popping out of that bubble and getting to know and hear our inner guide's direction, think outside of the bubble, and do what we love and are inspired to do.

How many of us push ourselves to take risks without letting anyone else's influence take over?

We will not grow, and our minds won't expand if we keep following the footsteps laid out in front of us by others. We won't have the unique life experiences that are possible to us if we don't take control of our environment and follow our inner guidance. To connect with ourselves, we have to let go of the thoughts and actions imposed on us by our external environment.

Some of us know all of this; we sense it but aren't willing to investigate and explore the other possibilities. And in not taking the time to change our personality, our environment, and our belief system, most of us are unconsciously inflicting the same damage and pain we've experienced growing up, over and over again, on our children and their children, down the genetic line, as well as our friends. Show me your top five friends, and I'll show you your future.

No wonder I numbed myself most of my life! Not a good solution of course, but at times, way better than dealing with what I thought was my only reality back then.

Line those shoes up girl, separate those clothes by color and fabric and clean those dishes right after dinner. Saturday is cleaning day. Get a toothbrush and scrub that grout around the shower. Dust before you vacuum. Eat everything on your plate; there are people starving in Africa. Be on time, mind your manners, hold the door, say God bless you, don't play in the rain, and save your money for a rainy day. Children should be seen and not heard. Shut up unless I tell you to talk. Stop crying before I give you something to cry about. Brush your hair this way. Nice girls don't dress like that.

You must work hard to make good money. The struggle is a part of life. Wear black at a funeral, don't wear white in the winter. Send Christmas cards. Call your mother. It's the right thing to do. It's the right thing to do!

But really, what is the right thing to do? Do they themselves know what the right thing to do is? Or is it just what they, and the people before, had been doing all their life and considered right?

I believe there is a huge spiritual disconnect with our inner guidance system; The Universe, Source, God, or whatever label feels best for you. Now I'm not saying that everyone is a zombie because I know a lot of successful, well-rounded, and educated humans that have managed to snap out of this psychological warfare and wake up. But YO, there are a lot of zombies walking around on this planet. It's like a plague!

I am just amazed at how our subconscious mind is unconsciously running the show most of the day. It's the memories, beliefs, fears, and subjective maps of reality that direct the course of what you do in your life without awareness. The subconscious mind is a program in the background of our brain that runs our physical body and involuntary actions 95% of our day, while our conscious mind runs only 5% of the day and is used mostly when we need to decide, critically think, or rationalize something.

The scary part is that most times, we don't even realize that we are unconscious. And that can become tricky when trying to navigate life on a day-to-day basis.

Take a moment to think about your day and your daily routines. Try this quick test to check if you are conscious or not. If you are right-handed, make a conscious decision to brush your hair and teeth with your left hand. It will be the hardest thing you've ever done, and I promise it will be a challenge unless you're ambidextrous because you will have to become conscious to complete this task. And if you get frustrated and switch back to your right hand because you don't have time or it's too hard, within seconds, you just default back into your subconscious program.

Doesn't that make you want to know everything you can about how to stay conscious? Are you a little curious?

We are mostly unconscious throughout the day unless there is an emergency or we have something new and interesting/outside of the box happening, and we don't even know it! Walking zombies doing the same things day after day, week after week, month after month, and **WE DON'T EVEN KNOW IT!** But to me, the worst part is answering the question of what kind of program we are running.

Conscious Mind

The conscious mind is only about 5 % of the total mind. It's made up of logic and reasoning as well as our creative abilities, which give rise to our free will. All things you are aware of, all mental processes and sensations of which you are aware. It takes care of all logical and intellectual thought processes.

Your conscious mind is your objective or thinking mind. It has no memory, and it can only hold one thought at a time. This mind has four essential functions. First, it *identifies* incoming information. This is information received through any of the six senses: sight, sound, smell, taste, touch, or feeling. Your conscious mind is continually observing and categorizing what is going on around you.

To illustrate, imagine that you are walking along the sidewalk, and you decide to cross the street. You step off the curb. At that moment, you hear the roar of an automobile engine. You immediately turn and look in the direction of the moving automobile to identify the sound and where it is coming from. This is the first function.

The second function of your conscious mind is *comparison*. The information about the car that you have seen and heard goes immediately to your subconscious mind. There, it is compared with all your previously stored information and experiences with moving automobiles.

If the car, for example, is a block away and moving at thirty miles per hour, your subconscious memory bank will tell you that there is no danger and that you can continue walking. If, on the other hand, the car is moving toward you at sixty miles per hour and is only 100 yards away, you will get a "danger" message that will stimulate further action on your part.

The third function of your conscious mind is *analysis*, and analysis always precedes the fourth function, *deciding*.

Your conscious mind functions very much like a binary computer, performing two functions: It accepts or rejects data in making choices and decisions. It can deal with only one thought at a time, positive or negative, "yes" or "no." This is why people who adopt positive thinking lifestyles regularly read and learn from inspirational quotes. Our single-track minds can only entertain one idea at a time, so keeping it occupied with uplifting material has the power to block negative thoughts.

The Subconscious Mind:

The subconscious mind is a secondary mind system that regulates everything in our life. In psychological terms, we **define the subconscious** as the part of our mind that is not currently in focal awareness. In simpler terms, it's the barrier our mind makes because the brain is continually receiving information through our senses.

However, this barrier is not blocking everything. It stores the information in the brain for later retrieval. You may have heard the saying that our mind forgets nothing. The subconscious acts as a filter so we're not overloaded with stimuli from our environment.

Examples of Subconscious Behavior

Sub-consciousness allows us to do things we don't have to think about, but we can alter them if we choose to. A good example of subconscious behavior is breathing. We don't have to think to breathe at all, but we can change how we control our breathing and its pattern.

Other examples of the subconscious are subconscious memory or automatic skills. Pianists or typists don't have to look at the piano keys or keyboard to know where the keys are. Automatic skills start as a learned skill, but as we repeat the movement, the executive function fades over time.

Resistance toward change is another example of subconscious behaviors. Survival is wired into our psyche, but sometimes our gut instincts may be harmful to us. Gut instincts are subconscious behavior that tells us what to do and what not to do. However, gut instincts can be wrong sometimes.

We may assume that finding happiness is good, but the change that we need to make to achieve that happiness may cause us fear and pain. Fear and pain are not necessarily bad, but our subconscious may tell us otherwise and thus deterring us from making that leap.

The Difference between Unconscious and Subconscious

The unconscious and the subconscious are two distinct phenomena. The unconscious is a process that happens automatically and is not available for introspection.

The subconscious, by contrast, is part of our consciousness process that is not actively in focal awareness.

Unconscious Mind:

When people have the same thoughts, do the same things, and live with the same emotions for so long, they are no longer conscious of those states of mind and body because they've become emotionally conditioned to the past or habituated into the same familiar future. This is when the body becomes the mind. The unconscious mind (or the unconscious) consists of **processes in the mind that occur automatically and are not available for introspection**. Although these processes exist beneath the surface of conscious awareness, they are thought to exert an effect on conscious thought processes and behavior.

A Mental process that is inaccessible or hidden traumatic experiences, memories that are too frightening to acknowledge. Most that go on in the mind is unconscious but can still impact your behavior. Most of what is in the unconscious mind got there through the process of repression. Repression describes a mechanism whereby we push unpleasant or unacceptable feelings, memories, or urges into our unconscious mind.

Example: Childhood abuse or rape. There is no memory of it, but the struggle to form relationships is real. Maybe someone was attacked by a dog at a young age and had no memory of this, but there is an intense phobia of dogs. Although the trauma is repressed, the symptoms experienced as adults are an expression of their trauma.

Prime Directive of the Unconscious Mind

- Stores memories. ...

- It's the domain of emotions. ...

- Organizes all your memories. ...

- Represses memories with unresolved negative emotions....

- Presents repressed memories for resolution. ...

- May keep the repressed emotions repressed for protection. ...

- Runs the body. ...

- Preserves the body. ...

Wakeup call: you've been programmed by The Parents, their parents, and even their parent's parents, and your environment, going back in time for who knows how long, and most of us have no clue.

It seems to me that we had very little control over our behaviors and patterns unless we woke up to the notion that someone downloaded the wrong software into our brains and got pissed off about it. And that might not ever happen unless you are older than about seven or thirty if you're lucky. That should piss anyone off! And for me personally, it's annoying to find this shit out at the age of forty-five. Yet, at the same time, finding this out now is way better than never.

So, unless you were one of the lucky ones who studied Quantum physics, epigenetics, and all that fancy science stuff, how would you even know? I knew at a very young age that something wasn't right, and I fought to be my true self, but that wasn't allowed because there were so many rules that The Parents and the rest of the world had.

A lot of things didn't make any sense to me for a while. The first half of my life, in all honesty, seemed like a rotten joke. I knew it was time to become someone else because the life I had so far was not even close to what I wanted, yet I felt guilty because maybe it was my karma.

"Maybe I did something horrible in the past, and I have to pay for it now. Damn, I must have been awful in my past life to experience so much trauma. And why am I still here? How am I still here? I don't even want to be here! But ending my life wasn't a choice anymore once my children were born."

After years of trying to "fix me" and doing everything wrong, I knew I had to make some high-level changes. At first, I just wanted to move to another country and start over, but I realized that I would still be bringing myself along, so that made no sense. I had a lightbulb moment one night at the ripe age of forty-five that changed my life, and I will forever be grateful for that little voice inside that demanded my attention and never gave up on me.

I was alone one night, randomly looking up into the sky, into the stars, and I swear on everything that a beam of light went straight into my mind, my 3rd eye, and within seconds, I decided to make a solid commitment to doing the complete opposite of almost everything I had ever done in the first forty-five years of my life.

I knew that I had to do something extreme at this point, and I didn't know how or what I was going to do, but I became obsessed and started investing all my free time, studying, taking notes on personal development, shadow work, energy work, epigenetics, journaling, meditating, understanding human behavior better, healing myself by removing animal products from my diet to eliminate medications, and physical fitness.

This work was a bit tedious, and there were many times when I wanted to quit, but instead, I gave myself small breaks and some time to heal while peeling away all the layers of personality and the pain I had acquired over the many years of my existence. This was a slow process in the beginning, and there were many days when I was mentally and emotionally exhausted, even physically sick, but I kept reminding myself that there was no future for me if I didn't take drastic action and work on the demons that haunted me every moment of every day.

I decided to re-wire myself and my brain and completely change my personality to no longer be the zombie I was trained to be but to be the human, the spirit, and the soul, that I truly felt lived deep within me. The voice inside was calling me in the moments when death seemed like a better option. It nagged me and would sometimes stop me in my tracks.

I wanted to believe it was some kind of special gift I had because I had experienced so many transcendental moments thus far, but my old programming and the opinions of other humans around me kept me on edge, wondering whether or not I was insane. After all, my life and my family were completely insane, so who's to say it didn't rub off on me?

Before I get started, I want to let you know a little about me and some general info that will make sense later here. I was born in 1967, the only redhead in my family with two younger brothers growing up in the '70s, '80s, '90s, and so on. Sometimes I am a lot, but I understand that we are always a work in progress. I grew up in Southwest Philadelphia and still like to use some slang here and there as I haven't reprogrammed my vocabulary completely. For this book, I decided to be exactly who I was and who I am now.

"I feel like Steve Harvey right now explaining why there may be some typos in here and that I am aware that my language is bad, but he is one of my long lists of great teachers, someone I admire tremendously, so it's all good..."

I'm hoping with all of my experiences, tragedies, and accomplishments that, I can help as many people as possible once I make it clear and explain to you through my story that no matter what the circumstance, no matter how shitty your life is, whether you're parents sucked, you were homeless, rich or poor, raped, promiscuous, boy, girl or confused, mommy issues, daddy issues, or disease, you still can have the life you want if you really want it, no matter what your age.

My story is brutal in some parts because I was in ridiculously abusive situations for the first half of my life. I was a very angry person inside and "a desperate-for-love-human-being" for a very long time until a switch went off in my head when I turned forty-five. The one thing this won't be is a hard read. I also want to say up front that I wish no ill will on any genetically related human beings and the people in my life that abused me, as I have been able to understand their programming and thought processes and move forward into my best life.

I understand that we are all energy, perfect souls in a human body, living a human experience. We are one. I look at all people now and remind myself that they were once someone's perfect, tiny, innocent baby, and I am choosing to use my story to help other people do the same. Everything I say here, though some of my family members may not enjoy or agree with it, is my truth, as we all interpret our experiences differently.

"You are the dream of all your ancestors."- Bert Hellinger

The so-called black sheep of the family are, in fact, hunters born of paths of liberation into the family tree.

The members of a tree who do not conform to the norms or traditions of the family system, those who since childhood have constantly sought to revolutionize beliefs, going against the paths marked by family traditions, those criticized, judged, and even rejected, are usually called to free the tree of repetitive stories that frustrate entire generations.

The black sheep, those who do not adapt, those who cry rebelliously, play a basic role within each family system. They repair, pick up and create new and unfold branches in the family tree.

Thanks to these members, our trees renew their roots. Its rebellion is fertile soil, its madness is water that nourishes, its stubbornness is new air, and its passion is the fire that re-ignites the light of the heart of the ancestors.

Uncountable repressed desires, unfulfilled dreams, and the frustrated talents of our ancestors are manifested in the rebelliousness of these black sheep seeking fulfillment. The genealogical tree, by inertia, will want to continue to maintain the castrating and toxic course of its trunk, which makes the task of our sheep difficult and conflicting work.

However, who would bring new flowers to our tree if it were not for them? Who would create new branches? Without them, the unfulfilled dreams of those who supported the tree generations ago would die buried beneath their own roots.

Let no one cause you to doubt; take care of your rarity as the most precious flower of your tree.

-   Bert Hellinger

CHAPTER 01 | THE PARENTS

My childhood was brutal. It was, in simple words, a series of many horrible moments and themes that stemmed from the limited conditioning, twisted behaviors, and personalities of "The Parents." Those parents were my parents, their parents, and so on and so forth, probably over a hundred generations back or more, if I am guessing right. There was a lot of mental, emotional, verbal, and physical abuse. The Parents divorced in 1979 when I was twelve. And that's when what I thought was bad became worse.

Honestly, I'm surprised I made it this far. I never connected with my family. I hated school and left home at seventeen, not too long after My Parents' divorce. I was a teenage runaway. My grandmother used to say I was a gypsy. To date (2022), I've moved over fifty times and been homeless more times than I can count.

Welcome to my story.

At the tender age of sixteen, I was molested and raped by two older men. My life was the typical scenario of a young girl with major daddy issues and an abusive family. As I got older, I was always attracted to the "bad boys." You might think that I should have known better after all that I had been through. But my attraction toward them had a sensible explanation.

Most of the nice boys I knew wanted me to be different. I was a loose cannon, a hot mess, an emotional wreck, but there was this propelling voice inside that kept pushing me, that wouldn't give up on me, and that wouldn't let me give up on myself even when I wanted to just die.

I was born out of wedlock in 1967. The Parents were nineteen-year-old teenagers and clueless. I call them "The Parents" because I have detached myself from them emotionally and physically and because my kids unknowingly gave me the idea for that title. I was never like my parents when I had to take on that role. Being one made me realize that I never received the love and affection I deserved as a child.

I don't see them as loving parents; I never did. I see them as a means, or a channel required to carry out my birthing process and nothing more. It may sound like I'm angry, but I'm not. I just know when to walk away from the people who rejected me and did not serve me. I'm 100% certain that nineteen-year-olds should not have babies, yet I am unsure if there really is an age that is reasonable as, in my experience, making this kind of commitment is one of the most important projects there will ever be in life.

But to The Parents and the rest of the DNA-connected humans in my bubble, having a female with red hair and freckles must have been an all-time shocker. I was the big secret, and I'll be damned if that little voice inside of me wasn't trying to show me as much as possible. But I was too disconnected and caught up in the web of lies, the magic show, and the all-time best seller to pay attention to what was really going on in my world.

One day, out of nowhere, it all hit me. My story is not just about all my sick experiences and drama; It's about recognizing how two people can make a baby and potentially ruin that child mentally and emotionally for the rest of their life without having a clue. It is about me figuring out that I had been brainwashed for the first forty-five years of my life until I had an awakening that changed everything.

To be fair, my parents were not involved as intensely with me after I left home. So, the environment and the people I attracted, with my one-way, negative, low-level energy programming, had a helping hand in my grooming as well.

I will say that now, I am very grateful for all my experiences, and I wouldn't change a thing other than opening my eyes maybe a little sooner and, for God's sake loving myself. I mean, I feel extremely blessed to have been taunted by my inner self to the point where I had no choice but to listen.

The scary question to me would be, what if I didn't listen? Where would I be right now? My guess would be dead in someone's closet somewhere. So, I'm sending love to the child in me who just wanted to have a loving, supportive family and feel special. You are beautiful, smart, courageous, talented, loyal, and trustworthy, just like all children. I love you and release you from all the pain I put you through. I didn't know that you couldn't have known what to do until you experienced these challenges and made real changes.

If you feel like you relate to this, send yourself some love; it's okay and necessary.

I was starving for affection from my mother and father, but it just wasn't in the script for me. The worst part was that I didn't understand why. I mean, if I knew that it had somehow been my fault, it may have made some sense. But instead, I kept hoping that it would change even as I got older, but it didn't.

My mother was a Catholic school graduate, who often reminded me that she wanted to be a doctor, but unfortunately, she got pregnant with me at nineteen. Those were her words. Her reminding me of this and making it sound like I was a "mistake" made me feel really bad for a long time and eventually started to piss me off deep down, even as I got older. But now, I believe we all can do or be whatever we want in life no matter what's in the way, so I was just a really bad excuse for her never being successful.

"See, children shouldn't be having babies."

I have compassion for her now because I understand some of her upbringings better and just see things more clearly, but that doesn't change my story of "The Parents."

My Mom was not affectionate at all. She was attractive, maybe about 5' 3" tall, with thick, dark black hair and dark brown eyes. She was smart, cold, distant, selfish, cocky, and narcissistic. Though I see her now with fewer words. She was sad and miserable. I always felt like she hated me, or I just wasn't good enough no matter what I did. Even when I was little, I felt the anger in her from a distance and all around me.

My guess now is that it had little to do with me and everything to do with her choices and her childhood. It's almost a big blur to me like she was running around in default mode, twenty-four-seven, not really feeling or caring, just doing what she was trained to do and what she thought she had to do.

Looking back now, after mimicking her behavior and conditioning for so many years, I suppose, for the most part, she lived in fear of my father and was pretty disappointed in her parents as well. She, too, didn't have a good relationship with her mother and wound up being just like her in the end.

But mainly, her life was all about her sons and the men she chose and still is. As a mother myself, I never could understand any of that. How do you pick one kid over another or love one more than the other and make it obvious to everyone around you? I mean, I have three kids, and they're all soooo different! Like poles apart. I love them all differently but not one more than another.

I realize now that The Parents both had a hard life, but I can't understand how any mother could separate herself from her child on purpose. Was she running her program unconsciously? It felt like she was competing against me. I know now that it was all she knew as I heard many stories of her mother doing the same thing to her and her sisters when she finally had her son after giving birth to three daughters and many lost pregnancies in between and after. It took years for me to grasp that one because, later in my teenage years, my grandmother was like a mother to me. They say with age comes wisdom, but as far as my mother and aunts are concerned, they don't even know my grandmother the way I describe her.

My father was a truck driver for food stores and a contractor on the side. He was 6' tall, with light brown hair and green eyes, the only thing we had in common. He had big, rough hands from building things and working. He was a liar and a thief and made no bones about it, but he was also handsome, and when he smiled, it lit me up. In all honesty, it was a big relief when he smiled. Most times, when he was home, he was physically abusive. He didn't really speak to us unless he was giving an order or beating the shit out of us.

He was a player with women, and if you had money, you were his best friend. I think he told me at least twenty times that he never wanted kids. He even told me this when I was in my 30s as if that would quantify or make up for being such a heartless dick to me most of my life. And to be honest, the only time he and I were a little bit close was when I had a lot of money if we were speaking.

He never asked me for anything back then, but it seemed like all of a sudden, he actually wanted to know me. I don't think there's anything wrong with surrounding yourself with moneymakers and successful people, but his personality was confusing. He's always put his friends before his family. And again, as I grow older and wiser, I know now that he was abused as well and adhered to nothing else.

My father would beat my brothers and me senseless, sometimes until we bled. Most of the beatings took place when he would randomly show up in the middle of the night after work. He had a routine of going through the whole house looking for dirt or disorder, and unfortunately, my mother was not a clean freak. In all fairness to her, she had three little kids that played with a lot of toys and got into everything, so things were always a mess.

But my father wasn't a rational human being. He was a broken man who didn't know how to love or be kind. The word patience was not in his vocabulary.

He would beat us so badly that all you could hear was my brothers and me screaming and crying for our lives. Imagine the sound of that chorus from three children under the age of maybe eight years old. Sometimes I had to wait in my bedroom in fear as he would go through my brothers' room breaking everything and throwing their things around as he lifted their mattresses and looked under their beds.

I would be on my knees organizing the shoes in my closet, shaking in fear. My mother would peep in and whisper, "you'd better hurry up, girl; you're next." But I was trained to be a clean freak, so when it came to my bedroom, I was usually good to go with a warning.

I know so many people who are proud and boast about how we kids who grew up in the 70s are better than the entitled kids of the world today because our parents beat the shit out of us, and we listened. Well, yeah, we listened because we feared for our lives, but I don't agree that beating a child is okay or the best way to make someone whose brain is not fully developed understand what you are trying to teach them while you are screaming, beating them, and breaking things.

And I wonder how many of them, us, would be considered mental patients and emotionally broken as adults from that abuse. Okay, so you learned how to put your shit away the way your parents taught you. You learned how to eat everything on your plate whether you liked it or not. You hold the door for people and say thank you, or God bless you when someone sneezes. Great! I wonder how many of us are now abusers like The Parents.

How many of us know how to sit down with a child, or even an adult for that matter, and have a civil, clear conversation? How many of us can sit down with a child and patiently listen to what they have to say? If you take the time to listen, children are really very smart, and their imagination is mind-blowing!

I know for sure that wasn't always easy for me. If my kid was freaking out or yelling, my knee-jerk reaction would be to freak out or yell. Basically, mirroring their behavior unconsciously.

I know from my own experience that it can be difficult to pull yourself away from the list of things that must get done in a day and take the time to listen, but children will always have something to say, whether they can articulate it correctly or not. And we are their teachers. Their voice matters. And if you want them to be just like you, all you have to do is be who you are.

I remember a plaque on my grandparent's wall that read, "children should be seen and not heard." This really was a thing back then and most likely still is because I'm sure it was passed down by The Parents in some unlucky child's world somewhere.

No child wants to be brutally abused, especially by the people who are supposed to love and protect them. Most children need more protection from The Parents than from a stranger on the street. It sometimes amazes me when a parent is worried that their child is hanging out with someone who they deem a bad influence, but my question is, are they worse than you?

Every child is born innocent and perfect. And in my opinion, the only hands that should be laid on them should be in a loving manner.

My mother and father were also damaged by The Parents and their environment and, to this day, probably "know not what they did" because they are trapped in the cycle. They are unable to identify the wrongs in their conduct, and it just keeps going.

I was starving for affection from my mother and father, but it just wasn't in the script for me, and I didn't understand it and hoped that this would change as I got older, but it didn't. I realize clearly now that in order for me to have a great life, I could not hold anyone hostage anymore for what they did or what I experienced in lieu of being around them because they, too, were experiencing life through their eyes and The Parent's eyes.

That was a hard one to swallow because, let's face it, isn't it easier to feel sorry for yourself and beat the drum of what was done to you and how it would have been different if it wasn't for "BLANK and what they put you through?"

How many of us have been on our knees asking, "Why is this happening to me?" What did I do to ever deserve this?" Did ya ever hate God? I did for a very long time. Hell, I didn't even believe in God.

But when diving down into my past and after much effort into working on my shortcomings, it doesn't faze me anymore. I am wiser now, and that's a good thing because we all have different eyes, and being able to see clearly is key.

No matter what happened with The Parents as I grew up, the beginning of my childhood was pretty great. Back in the early 70s, it was normal to get up at six am, watch cartoons, then go outside and play for hours. For the most part, we rarely came back home until the streetlights came on. We rode our bikes for hours all over the place; we built the best forts out of old boxes and rocks or snow; we played street ball barefoot, hide the belt, red light-green light-yellow light-stop. We climbed trees and played in nature. It's the same story for all Gen-Xrs.

I was very much a tomboy and loved hanging out with boys. Probably because I had two brothers and I liked sports, but mainly because I hated girl drama even when I was young. But eventually, there came a time when I just felt the urge to sing and dance. It was my calling; something inside me that I couldn't explain, and I would immerse myself in music for hours, singing to my heart throb Shawn Cassidy posters or in my mirror.

I would get together with some of my girlfriends and write out a show. We would put notes on our neighborhood friend's doors that read something like "Showtime at Madeline's garage, eight am for ten cents." The cool thing was that we had an audience that actually paid. I was a tiny entrepreneur before I turned ten. No one's parents ever came out to look for them. Some parents would ring a bell or whistle at dinner time, but that was pretty much it. The only time my mother would call me was when she needed me to go to Mary's store for cigarettes and bread or maybe her favorite cookies.

I hated going to Mary's store because she had two gigantic German Shepard dogs always running around loose. They would be behind the counter protecting Mary, which was great for her as she was a little, white-haired old lady by herself. But those dogs wanted to eat me, and that scared me shitless. And if I didn't go to the store for my mother, she would put a major guilt trip on me like, fine, don't expect me to pay for your dance classes anymore, girl.

All the kids would be in each other's houses eating whatever we could find whenever we could. My favorite was going to Madeline's house because her mother made the best meatballs! She must have cursed me out time and time again because I'd eat at least four of them any time I could. Those days were the opposite of today's world, and I'm truly grateful for every experience.

There were some creepy people around as well. And I guess that's where my disgust for men first started. It was a typical day if I walked to the store to get my mother cigarettes and bread and had some older guy yell and *woohoo* at me driving by. This started around the age of nine. One day I was out trick or treating and came up on a neighbor's house, this old guy Felix. Felix used to give all the kids the King size candy bars, and he would ask me to come back the next day so he could teach me rummy, the card game.

He said he would give me a dollar every time I won, so I took him up on that because penny candy at Mary's store was a big deal, dogs and all. I noticed when I arrived the next day that his wife was not there. He said she went bowling. I wasn't in the house for five minutes when he would try to make out with me. I was maybe eight or nine. This is a seventy-five-year-old man with some greasy hair strips, thick bottle cap glasses, and, sorry, just gross. He could have represented the Lolli-pop gang.

I didn't know what the F was going on, but I clenched my teeth shut as he outlined my mouth with his tongue, holding my face tightly with both hands. I just prayed that he would stop and play rummy, for God's sake. As I look back on this and replay it all, I almost had the attitude of, "let's just get this over with, k?" That is not a great mindset for such a young little girl. I think Felix got the hint for about a minute, and we would play. He would let me win and give me a dollar, and so on. When it was time to leave, he would sit me down, give me a soda and some candy, and talk to me about butterfly kissing. WTF is butterfly kissing? I still, to this day, don't know, but I can take a guess. He made a move, and I bolted out the door. Jesus H Christ, wtf is wrong with people? I never went back, and I never told anyone because I thought I would get beat.

I guess this is at least one problem with people not checking on their kids. Not too long after that, while walking to the park to play baseball, there was a guy sitting on a bench by the swings in shorts with his penis hanging out down to his knee. At such a young age, my thoughts were always, "OMG, men are fucking gross." Between all that, the fact that my dad was big into porn and hustler magazines freaked me out, so I didn't have the best feelings or respect for men, to say the very least.

I really didn't know much about any of this stuff until our mailman was stealing the neighbor's mail and calling the mothers on the street to let them know he was watching their daughters. That was the time when my mom took my anatomy book from school to explain penises and vaginas. UGH! I had no idea what the heck she was telling me. I was nine, but I guess she did her best. Either way, nothing was better than the freedom I had in nature and playing with my friends.

I went to Catholic school from first to seventh grade. I had some teachers but mostly nuns, who made a habit of beating little children in front of the class. I remember one kid named Gary in second grade who did something wrong at recess outside, and when we all sat down to class, two nuns came in with a big metal trashcan and lid. They put it at the front of the class, called Gary up, and made him get in that trash can. I can't even explain what was going through my mind, but it was a horrible feeling.

After Gary got in, his face bright red and scared shitless, they made him squat down and place the metal lid on top, then proceeded to slam the lid and violently shake the big metal trashcan back and forth with this child in it. It was brutal, and I've always wondered how Gary's mental state would be as an adult. I know for sure that I never "shook" that memory.

I got in trouble so many times that I lost count, mostly for not paying attention. I mean, when you're up all night getting the shit beat out of you or listening on your knees into the floor vents as your parents are screaming back and forth, it's kind of hard to sleep then have a good day at school, but no one ever asked if I was okay, they just beat me. I had a teacher, Mrs. S, who used to lock me up in the stationary closet with the light out during the class period because I answered a question incorrectly or was on the wrong page as I was a daydreamer.

She would grab my hair and pull it back and forth until my entire brain was pulsing, then she'd make me go outside of the classroom, put my hands behind my back, chin, and nose to the wall, and stand there until class was over.

I was in fifth grade when I first began cutting class. I had piano lessons for an hour on Wednesdays in the convent of my school. My mom would put $5.00 in an envelope to give to Sister Peter Marion, but after about three lessons, I became tired of getting my knuckles beat with a ruler because I messed up on my assignment, so I would cut piano lessons on Wednesdays and shoot down to the cafeteria and spend those five bucks on a bottle of coke and some choco-sticks or whatever candy I could afford.

I absolutely hated catholic school, but I always got straight A's, so no one asked any questions. Back then, if you got beat by a nun or teacher, the last thing you wanted to do was tell The Parents because they would beat you for getting beat.

So, in a nutshell, getting beat by adults was a thing back in the 70s, and no one did anything about it. That's just the way it was, and we all put up with it because we were conditioned to believe that it was normal and that we deserved it. And we were little and afraid.

Towards the end of The Parent's marriage, the final straw for my mother finally happened. Late one night, after my father beat her, got ready for his date, and left, she tossed some clothes in a few big bags and got us into the car. We had no idea what was going on, and my only question was, "what about Liebe, my dog?" Liebe was our miniature schnauzer that came from the next-door neighbor's litter. He was small, silver, and white and just a great dog.

I could tell my mother was very nervous as she bolted down the street, taking us to my aunt's house in Northeast Philadelphia. We stayed there for about a week, and it was the first time I felt at peace in a while. We didn't ask questions; we just did what we were told. I remember my father calling a few times asking where we were and my aunt playing dumb to protect us. He called my grandmother and threatened that if we didn't come back, he was going to make her life hell.

After about a week, I suppose, out of fear, my mother took us back home. I don't think my aunt was going to be able to house all of us, so she probably didn't have any other options back then. As we pulled up to our house, it looked like everything we owned was chopped up with an axe and displayed over our entire front lawn. I felt like I was in a movie as my experience was in slow motion while my mother pulled up to the curb to park the car. Dishes, furniture, clothes, toys, Easter baskets, and the axe are all over the lawn and sidewalk for everyone to see. All I could think of was to grab my Easter baskets and find my dog, Liebe.

Not too long after we arrived, my father's family was at our house. I guess my mother called them in fear, so they all swooped over, passing judgment and orders as always and controlling my father so he wouldn't kill anyone.

And not long after that began the divorce discussion. For me, that discussion took about three minutes. I had no idea what they meant by divorce, but I'll never forget the day my father left. He ordered me to go to Mary's and bring back cigarettes, then he was gone, and I was devastated.

CHAPTER 03 | THE DIVORCE IS FINAL

It was one week before Christmas in 1979. The Parents' divorce is final, and my mom moves us to Upper Darby, Pennsylvania, the suburbs. We didn't know it at the time, but she bought a house with a guy she worked with and was dating on the down low. I guess you do what ya gotta do. I would not have wanted to be in her shoes at that time.

The only way I can describe moving from Southwest Philly to Upper Darby back then is like this; I was glittery, bubbly, very broken emotionally, abused, and not in any way mature at almost thirteen years old, leaving Catholic school, leaving my home, my parents divorcing, relocating to a dreadful area in my mind, and losing all of my childhood friends; cause back then you could only write letters and call on the house phone.

I was allowed to ride my bike, but we were like thirty minutes away from my old neighborhood by car. Life was different back then. I'm forced to start in a new middle school with people who wear flannel shirts and corduroy pants with furry boots and listen to rock and heavy metal. I love that shit now, but not when I was in my pre-teens. Worse of all, I was still listening to Debbie Boone and Shawn Cassidy or my favorite song by the Silver Convention, Fly Robin, Fly, and Donna Summer. I was clearly different.

Everyone smoked cigarettes or weed, and most did drugs or drank beer in the mornings on the hill in the park before they got to class. It was frightening to me to start this new school. I did NOT fit in at all. I was a quiet, emotionally challenged, skinny redhead with freckles and jacked-up teeth with an

Italian last name. They called me bucky beaver. In fact, my own brother D called me that for years.

Back then people would say "blood is thicker than water," but I found out later the hard way that blood doesn't mean squat. It just means you have similar blood, or at least some of us are told that lie. The notion that blood is thicker than water is often touted, but it's a myth unless you're Italian or think you are Italian (this is a Philly thing). Most people who grew up in my neighborhood did not take the same DNA test that I took a few years ago as a joke to clarify things.

In my opinion, it's impossible to be 100% anything, and in Philly, the vast majority of families identified as Italian or claimed to have Italian heritage. It's pretty remarkable, really. I only discovered the true meaning of my mother's frequent admonition that "you're not Italian, trust me," fifty years later.

Whoo-Waa-what? I'll get to that later too. It's amazing how easily we just believe whatever people tell us. The question is, why wouldn't you believe your family?

I digressed again as my mind was trying to process this mindless chatter that made me think even more. It's quite annoying and can make you nuts if you let it, but you can absolutely change that.

Anyway, back in our new environment, Upper Darby, one week into the divorce, here I am, dressed like a disco ball, praying on the long ass walk to my new school that I would survive this torture. I mean, I was in my head, but really, come on, who would blame a child for being mental at this point?

I was bullied big time A LOT, and the people in that area were really racist and mean. I remember in eighth grade, my teacher would make fun of my white cowboy boots with purple fringe. Which, by the way, were pretty awesome! I used to wear beads in my hair, and the boys would pull them out during class. Beads all over the floor. Each time one dropped, my heart dropped as if each landing was big!!.

This place was severely different from where I came from. I mean, my parents were, and probably are still, racist and judgmental hoo-haz, nauseating to say the very least, but it was unhinging to see people act so mean-spirited. I remember a family that moved in a few houses down from us and lasted maybe two weeks because the neighbors disgracefully stoned their home until they left. Now I was a kid and didn't know all the details, but word on the street was that my new neighbors didn't like the color of their new neighbor's skin.

What happened to love thy neighbor? Would Jesus do this? WTF is wrong with people? Conditioning belief system again! But my family was no better. There were so many terrible names for anyone of another race, color, or religion. I'll ask this again, "would Jesus do this?" I will probably get shit for this, but I learned everything racist from my family at the dinner table. But it wasn't who I wanted to be.

That's the great thing about kids; they don't judge anything unless they are taught to or brainwashed into it. None of us were born racist or unkind. And honestly, I feel like you really have to work at being so damn ugly.

Most of the girls in my new school hated me as well. Welcome to Beverly Hills Jr. High. Sounds like a great school, a cool name, naa. I used to get notes from a group of girls telling me I was a scum bag and dead after school. They would all sit at my lunch table and stare at me and talk about the beating I was going to get. But I told the teacher, yes, I told my teacher, and she put an end to that, thank God. This Catholic schoolgirl was scared to death!

Either way, they found out and called me a rat. There's no winning here. They would wait outside the school for me and stare me up and down, give me the finger, etc. I think I did them a favor, though, because my shit was psycho, but nobody knew it yet...

Eventually, I got myself some corduroy pants and some Levis. I tried the furry boots, but yea, no, that didn't last long, not my style. So, I just did me, and they learned to deal with it. And over time, I made friends there and in my neighborhood. But they still tortured me. I was really quiet back then and to myself, but my mind raced constantly, and I was failing school. The stress of the divorce, the drama with my mother and her friends, not seeing my dad or maybe seeing him here and there but having to deal with my mean family was too much for me.

It was the beginning of the end of my education back then, but I did try. I went from being an A student in Catholic school to lowering my artistic skills by changing E's into B's on my report card with a pencil. My mom never knew. I no longer cared, and it only got worse.

By now, I was convinced that I was going to be a famous singer and eventually got the kahunas to audition for Al Albert's show. That's pretty funny. I practiced my Debbie Boone song, "You Light Up My Life," for weeks. I had never been on a real stage before, but I loved to sing. Long story short, after I fell in the street on my ass on my way to get my mom a pack of cigarettes before we got there, I auditioned, but about twenty other kids sang the same song.

When I finished, Al Alberts said, "you sounded ok, but you're very nasally." I was absolutely heartbroken. I guess I was around fourteen or so when we had auditions for the school talent show. What was I thinking? Ugh, so I signed up to sing a song. I had no idea what my next step would be, but it all just kinda played out. There was a girl in my class named Olympia; she was great. She would cheer me on and say, "you gotta sing Pat Benatar" over and over again with so much energy. I had no idea who Pat Benatar was at the time, but I listened and learned one of her songs, Hit me with your best shot.

A rumor got out in school that the new girl was in the talent show, and eventually, I got offers from random kids that played in bands to join them. And that's when I was in my first band with all my new Greek friends. I eventually cut all my hair off in my bathroom to look like Pat Benatar, had some band practices with the guys, and did the talent show. Funny, my mother never said a word about me cutting off about eight inches of my hair. No one did, to be honest. I was pretty invisible.

I remember how scared I was. OMG! My mom was on one side of the auditorium, and my dad was on the other. I was so excited to see my dad there that I ran up to him after to ask if he liked it. His only words were, "I couldn't hear shit." Honestly, that's all he said. Very sad indeed.

That was the beginning of my rock band life. After that talent show, I found myself drawn to different musicians all of the time. I played here and there at one of my close friend's houses, trying to learn the B52s and music that I'd never heard before, but it was cool. I felt so comfortable around musicians and soon realized that music was my true passion.

The Parents were divorced one week before Christmas in 1979, and the Sunday visitations began. My Dad was supposed to come every Sunday but didn't make most of them. He was living in New Jersey with his girlfriend Diana, the ride was over an hour, and he did try, but my guess is that he didn't know what the hell to do with all three of us. Probably because he never really spent any time with us growing up.

Every time he did come, my mom made sure to yell out the door, "where's my child support," and of course, they would just yell back and forth from the front door across the street where he parked.

To anyone who is in the middle or end of a divorce and has children, do not fight with your ex or talk shit about them in front of your kids. You will regret it for years because kids, never forget how you speak of the other parent. Kids hear everything. Tattoo this on your body!

Most of the time, my dad would take us to his parent's house. My grandparents on my dad's side were awful to us!!! This is back when everyone smoked cigarettes in the house and had plastic covers on their furniture that were stained yellow from the smoke. We would come in, take our shoes off and sit on the plastic couch until we were allowed in the kitchen, which was five feet away. My grandfather would sit on his recliner in front of the TV and say ZERO, he never spoke! If I went to give him a kiss hello, he would turn his head away.

Many years later, after his passing, my aunt D told me a little about his childhood and how his family was poor, and that they struggled. She said before his transition that he told her that he didn't know his kids loved him, so it kinda made sense thirty years later. I tried many times to speak with my grandfather, but he just didn't speak to us. I tried to hug or kiss him, but I guess he didn't know how to handle that. Maybe that was why my father was the way he was.

When my grandfather was on his deathbed, I made a point to visit him. I was much older then and figured it was the right thing to do. I did love him either way and wanted him to know that. The day I went over to visit, I was really nervous that he would reject me again, but to my surprise, he was very nice to me. Though it was brief, it was the best feeling in the world, and he soon passed.

It's heartbreaking to know that someone suffered all their lives in silence, never really knowing if they were loved. Never really knowing how to communicate their feelings. My grandfather didn't need to speak for me to feel the sadness in his heart. I don't know the story of his family, but I am sure that there were some pretty lame belief systems there.

My father had three sisters and a brother. The aunt we dealt with the most was Aunt Iz. When I was a child, I felt like she was an unhappy, mean-spirited human. She was very cold and blunt, but occasionally, and once in a while, she would say something funny. When she would voice her opinion and say something mean and way out of line, she'd always follow it up with, "well, it's the truth." I couldn't understand why she was still living at home at like forty years old. And I never saw her with a boyfriend until she was maybe in her fifties or sixties.

I can fill these pages with the nasty things she would say to us, mostly me. She was intimidating, mean, and judgmental. I was so afraid of her yet wanted her to love or accept me desperately, yet she didn't, and I didn't know why. She could even make my dad back down, but now she is much older and doesn't even recognize me. I feel bad for her because I can't imagine being so unhappy my whole life. Unfortunately, I found out years later that Iz had a mental breakdown and did some unspeakable, violent things that landed her in the psych ward for a bit, but she's back to living her life now. I wish her the best.

This is the shit that stuck with me for over fifty years. This is what I was made to believe was normal. Every once in a while, a kind part of their personalities would come loose, but not often. I realize that they had deeper issues, but it doesn't erase the memories. Now, I see things differently. It's actually very sad, and I have empathy for all of them, and quite literally fully except and believe, that if I want to be free from this fucking hell trap that I am living in, I have to let it all go!

Easier said than done for sure, and writing-this bestseller book is my final step to LETTING IT ALL GO!

I was a child, but these people, my family supposedly, constantly put me down. They would ask us over and over again at the dinner table, "who's your mom sleeping with now"? "Why is your hair like that? You destroyed your hair; what a shame." Jesus, I couldn't even eat food with my left hand because then I was "pretending" to be able to use both hands, and it wasn't allowed. The nasty rotten things they would say to us were just brutal and disturbing.

And they were all racist, so if you weren't white or Italian, they had something to say about that as well. When in fact, as I type this right this second, none of them are full-blood anything!

I can't tell you how many times my grandmom would say, "you better not come home with a big belly girl," or you're gonna be a whore like your mother," yet she was pregnant with my dad at sixteen!!! I was too skinny, they felt sorry for me because my teeth were so jacked up, and the list of things wrong with me went on and on. I didn't have the balls back then to say anything to any of them.

I feared them all, but eventually, when I got older, I went to visit my grandmother on a whim. I simply felt the need to say hi to her, I missed her, but she felt it important to spend twenty minutes putting me down that day, so I walked out in tears.

She yelled for me to come back, so I told my grandmother exactly how I felt about her. I told her that she was mean and rotten, and I'll never understand what I did to her that was so awful that she would treat me so badly, and then I walked out of her house.

"It's paralyzing when you are being abused by people you love and who are supposed to love you. It's so hard to take a deep breath and walk away because you're trained to believe you have to put up with it. And crazy enough, I still miss my grandmom and aunt to this day."

Eventually, when my dad felt more comfortable in his new relationship, he started bringing us to his girlfriend Diana's house. She tried her best with us. She was the first person to ever hug me and say I love you; she was very affectionate with all five of her kids and included me in everything. But she wasn't happy. After many years we had a conversation over lunch where she told me that she was lonely.

Again, even with her, my dad was never really around, at least not while I was there. Diana would cook like crazy for Thanksgiving and Christmas.

I have to say that being at her house for the holidays was some of the best times I can remember. They prepared big, wonderful meals, and the house was always packed with family. My two brothers and I would be there with Diana and her five kids, and about twenty minutes in, my dad would leave just before everyone sat down to eat because he had to work. I hated that he would just leave us there.

I used to feel so bad for Diana. She'd cook all day and make the holidays such a great time with great memories, but my dad never sat down for a second and appreciated her. Diana did a lot for her kids and for us. She had a pretty cool trailer, a big tent that fits a small dresser, and a double mattress in it at the campgrounds in New Jersey during the summer. My Dad would drive us there and dump us off. But I enjoyed my time with my stepsisters.

In the middle of the night, we would slowly unzip the tent and sneak out to get stupid. My stepsister Chrissy and I were close in age, so we got along pretty well. Chrissy had her older sister's ID, so we would walk out of the campground down to the liquor store and get two bottles of Boones Farm, Strawberry Hill, at $1.00 a bottle.

We'd head back to the campgrounds and just roam around drinking cheap strawberry wine. Chrissy usually had a joint or two on her, so at around thirteen, I started smoking weed and cigarettes with her and then with my brother D at home. My brother D and I are eighteen months apart, so we were pretty close when we were little. God, I have so many fun memories with them and some not-so-fun but normal stuff.

Eventually, I wound up moving in with Diana. I thought my dad lived there, but unknowingly he had a house down the shore that needed a lot of work at the time, so Diana felt it best I didn't stay there. Diana was a tiny, beautiful, black-haired, brown-eyed, single Italian woman with five children from her first marriage. And with a fingertip missing from her job on a printing press, she still managed to play the piano with such ease. I lived with Diana and her kids for about nine months or so full-time. And my two brothers went down the shore with my dad. It was a big change for me and the first time I had lived with females who were close to each other and cared about each other.

I don't know how long my brothers D and S stayed at my dad's, but I often heard that my dad was never there and that the neighbors took care of them. I felt bad for my brothers when I found out that they were there working on our dad's house every day after school while he was gone. The neighbors were in their seventies and very kind, but there was only so much they could do. My brothers were little boys. S was about five years younger than me, with blonde hair and big blue eyes. He was a good kid, as far as I remember.

I can't imagine what that must have been like for them at such a young age. I mean, I guess it was a good thing that our dad had nice neighbors who wanted to chip in. But let's face it; he did not know what he was doing.

The fact that I don't even know what my brother's lives were like seems strange to me. But again, I lived in a bubble too, and

I was in constant survival mode, so I couldn't see much of the real world.

It's crazy that I loved my dad so much but feared him at the same time. As I got older, there still was no connection between us other than the idea, or well, the very fact that he was my dad. He wouldn't reach out to me, but if I called, he would kind of speak with me. Three months after my first son was born, I had to call him and ask when he was going to come by and meet his grandson. He responded by explaining that he had to work which was his default answer/excuse for everything, so I lost it and cursed him out.

I felt the need to remind him of our relationship as I was very jealous of the connection he had with my stepsisters. I don't think they felt the same way about my dad as he did them, but it was very obvious that he was "crushing" on two of them.

"I am your only Fucking daughter, and you can't find an hour to meet your grandson?" I hung up and was very angry, but he called back and mentioned that it wasn't okay for me to curse at him. He eventually managed to take some time off his busy schedule, an hour, to be specific, to meet his grandson.

Haha, that's so funny to me! I can't curse at my parents. Who wrote that law? I'm not advocating that it's normal to curse your parents out. And I almost feel annoyed to even write this out because they were the ones who taught me that language. If you don't want your kids to curse, don't curse in front of them. I always wondered why my dad didn't want to be around me though he made it clear for years, over and over, that he never wanted kids. Nice!

My stepmom, Diana, did everything for us. My Dad never married Diana, but I always looked at her as the mom I never had. At the time, I wasn't sure why she took us on, but she did. I appreciate her and have missed her very much since she passed. As I got older, I had to ask her why she was with my dad. She was so unhappy, he was never around, and when he was, well, it wasn't enough. Unfortunately, he had banged her up a few times here and there as well, but she still hung around. I know that everyone must have noticed it, but I never heard anything about it. Diana said to me, "I'm in my sixties; who's gonna want me?"

I told her you're never too old be happy, and I'd say it again to anyone and everyone who will listen.

I became close to Diana's kids and my stepfamily in different ways because we spent a lot of time together. I can remember fondly the long drives home from Wildwood, New Jersey, to Upper Darby, PA, in the back of my dad's old, brown pickup truck with blankets over us and our bags holding them down from the wind. I loved being in the back of that truck. Obviously not so safe, but I think the '70s and '80s were just a different time.

Suffice it to say that those were the best years as far as kids having the most freedom from social media and TV.

We were always in nature. That's probably what kept us from getting in trouble but in time, that all changed, and eventually, I found myself running away with some random new friends living in their car for about two weeks until I could manage to find my aunt TC's farmhouse in Mullica Hill New Jersey. I stayed in a back room on the couch for a while, but no one even noticed that I was there. I couldn't stand my dad and his yelling, and I couldn't handle the fact that he wasn't there with me at all, as usual. And it bothered me how much attention he gave my stepsisters, yet he wouldn't even look at me.

CHAPTER 06 | ABUSE RANT, THE CHAIN CONTINUES

People don't like change, and they fear the unknown. People often find comfort in the familiar and the status quo. This can be particularly true when someone is different from most. They don't like it if you're different, as it challenges people's preconceived notions and can cause discomfort. There can be resistance to accepting and embracing differences, even when they are ultimately beneficial.

I believe that we all have a calling inside of us to be exactly who we are, but again, most would shut that voice off because it's simply not worth the aggravation and judgment they would have to endure had they shared it. Not all people are blinded, of course, so I'll just say the ones I know. My best affirmation was that I was the black sheep of this family.

Probably not a bad thing, and most likely not the best thing to keep repeating to myself or out loud. Now I watch my words.

I had to embrace the idea that there was something wrong with me, but I know better now that I wasn't the problem. I took all of those experiences with me my whole life. I was so conditioned and angry. It was sickening, and all of the things I hated the most about my family, I saw in myself until one day, literally in a moment, I woke up.

I watched my friends in Philly and their families. They all seemed so close and so happy, and I always wished that I could have a family like theirs. I wanted a family that said I love you and hugged each other and sat together at dinner. A family that played games together or even watched TV together.

But I didn't have those options and was forced to deal with that reality, and I somewhat adjusted to that life but hated it.

It's F'd up. We all just unconsciously slither into whatever vibration or energy is closest to us, even if it's not anything that we want at all. Even if we absolutely hate it. But as the Laws of the Universe say, like attracts like. The kind of thoughts and attitudes you have will attract events similar to them or on a similar vibration, which will make them a reality.

We literally separate from our inner being, our life force, our personal, customized GPS when we are not conscious and in the flow of well-being. But most of us are so addicted to our emotions from the past, living in the past, hypnotized by the past. Walking around like programmed zombies running on a program that someone else picked! When I was a kid, I just did what I was told, like a good soldier, mainly out of fear. Why? Because we are all programmed.

Hey, I'm not a scientist, and I don't play one on TV or have all of the answers, but I will say out loud that it's pretty fucked up!

It's brainwashing, and the brainwashers are brainwashed by other brainwashers who were brainwashed by their brainwashers, and so on. *Whew, say that twenty times fast.* The chain continues. They don't know any different, but they sure as hell believe that their way is the only way! And here's the thing that's even more fucked up; most of us can sense the difference between right and wrong, but it's easier to stay brainwashed than to use your voice or to do the work on yourself and change your mindset. What are we so afraid of?

Are we afraid of getting beat up? Afraid of words from someone who is probably unhinged? Come on. You know that person who drives you nuts is unhinged right? But you still go back for more. Why? Why do we care so much about what others think about us?

We all know deep down in our gut when people or things are not right, but to step outside of the box and be different, to trust your gut instead of settling for what we know or feel uncomfortable with, ehh, most likely ain't happening. And when you're around adult bullies who "supposedly" love you, and they probably do according to how much love they are actually capable of, and are your family, you are aligned with the massive challenge stars...

Abuse is a vicious cycle, and it should never exist. And I'm still not sure what the real game is. Are these experiences good for us? Are they supposed to make us stronger? Are the lessons a learning game? Is this considered the earth game? If I choose A, will I have an easier life than if I choose B? Red pill, blue pill? I've often heard that you pick your parents and decide your journey before you come here. So, as I go back in time, it looks like I wanted a real challenge.

Without sounding woo-woo, I've had many out-of-body experiences, i.e., astral projection, and they were all and always are, very specific and very real. And every time I experience these adventures, I download more information and gain a better understanding of why we are here.

In 2016 during a meditation and my first time experimenting with automatic writing, three tall men with long white beards dressed in long gowns came to me in the middle of what seemed to be a war. I was running around my old neighborhood in fear as I watched bombs go off and chaos all around me. I didn't need a dream dictionary for this one. And visuals are different for everyone. If you were fed that God has a big white beard and long hair, then that's most likely your mind's vision of God. If you pray to cows and call them God, then I suppose you would see cows.

To get to the point, the three men floated to me, lined up horizontally. In the background was my old neighborhood with bombs going off, explosions everywhere, people running, and people dying, and it was getting dark outside. The middle guy seemed to be the leader, and his name was Abraham. He gently placed his palm under my chin and lifted me into the air and above his head. He asked me telepathically when I was going to figure this all out.

He told me I had repeated this cycle seven times. He didn't hurt me, and I wasn't afraid. I felt like I instinctively knew who he was. He meant something to me, but I couldn't put my finger on it, and at the same time, I was mesmerized by his presence and was pretty happy to see him. With my eyes closed, my hand drew out the scene, my three guides, and their names. Since then, I've seen Abraham more and more in my visions and my mind's eye and communicate with him or the essence of him daily.

I've always known that I've been here many times, and this confirmed it for me. I felt I had three main guides, but I didn't know their names until then. This wasn't the final wake-up call for me. It was a nudge.

Six months after The Parent's divorce, my mother re-married in 1980 to a guy named Bongo. Yeah, soak it in. I don't know all of the facts; I was thirteen by then, but she married a guy who I thought was kind of nice at first. He was about 6' 5" tall and at least 300 pounds. He was a big dude! I was a good kid, and I loved everyone. And if my mom said this is my new husband. He's paying the bills, be nice, then I was nice. I feel like I need to salute right now. Hut234Hut

 I didn't know shit. I had almost thirteen years with the same two parents and the same bullshit over and over. How could anyone understand this next level at such a young age? My brother D was only eighteen months younger than me, and my brother S was, I think, four or five years younger. It must sound crazy that I still, to this day, don't really remember ages, dates, and time frames but I think I found a way to deal with everything by not dealing with it at all.

While my mom was just getting started in her new marriage, she became more and more disconnected from me. I can't speak for my brothers, but she and I had a strained relationship. She didn't talk to me, look at me, or acknowledge me. She was doing her, period. There was a lot of drinking going on and parties and, of course, drugs, but I could see that Bongo was not coping well. And soon, the new drama began.

He used to be away a lot. I think he worked on a ship or something like that. I'm not completely sure, but he would be gone for months at a time. I liked him and his family, but it was forced too soon, it was all just so much, but we did what we were told like good little soldiers.

In the meantime, I was still trying to adjust to the new school, the loss of my childhood friends, my parents breaking up, trauma, and being a teenager at the same time with zero guidance. I don't think Bongo had a clue as to what he was getting himself into. He didn't have kids, but now he has three that are not his blood, and we were young.

"There's the blood thing again."

My mom clearly wasn't ready for this shit, but I guess she did what she had to do. My mom and Bongo hung out with the people they both worked with who happened to all work at my uncle's business, where just about everyone did drugs and drank hardcore. My brother D worked for my uncle for a while, and I worked with them as well here and there when he would have sidewalk sales.

There was a time when my brother D left home in 1982-83 to live with my aunt and uncle, mom's side. I don't know why he left or what his story was, but he got out for a good amount of time until my mom eventually came for him when she was ready, I guess. I thought he was so lucky to be out of this hell hole, and I loved my aunt and uncle, but, in all reality, I never asked and never really knew what was going on with my brother D.

My aunt and uncle used to have a lot of great barbeques at their house on the farm. They would have pig roasts with tons of people, music, drugs, and booze. My uncle would play guitar with his family, who also played banjo and tambourine, and I would just sit with them and sing. I was innnnnn my glory! I just loved being there.

-Side note: my aunt didn't do drugs. 

I remember meeting one of their friends named Rutt at a party there, who seemed like a nice guy. One day Rutt came over to BABYSIT me. Rutt was the cool older guy at my uncle's parties that I connected with. Little did I know he had an ulterior motive. He talked to me as if I was a human being with meaning, so I trusted him and never thought for a minute he would be another disgusting male. I'm gonna take a stab and say he was probably around thirty to thirty-five.

Rutt came over to babysit one day, which was weird to me at that time, I mean, I'm thirteen now and cool, right, but we did what we were told to do, and The Parents left for a date. I'll never forget Rutt closing the door behind them. Within seconds, he leaned up against the door blocking the entrance asking me for a hug. My gut immediately went into knots, but I hugged him as he suggested, with his arms wide open and a smile, because ok, it's Rutt. And then came the dreaded follow-up.

"I love hugging you. Do you want to see what you did to me?"

Somehow, I instinctively knew what he meant. (As he looked down at his crotch) "Do you want to see my hard-on? Look what you did to me. "WTF? Again, I was thirteen. I'll just get to the narrative to follow for the rest of my days with my mom and her friends from when they returned home...

As I am writing and reading this, all I can hear in my mind is an old-school typewriter clicking in the background like an old news commercial.

"Mom, Rutt tried to show me his penis. He said I made him get that way."

Mom's default response was, "You're a liar. He would never do that."

Family meeting to follow with Rutt's best friend, my new stepdad Bongo, "Rutt said he would never do that."

I, fighting for myself: "How could I even come up with this shit?"

Ending: "Girl, you're a liar."

"I can't believe you would make something like this up." To be fair, this is not word for word, I'm 55 as of yesterday, 01/23, and there are some things I simply blocked out, but it's the nicest way I can find to explain it all. Bottom line, that was my first encounter with my mom's male friends acting like a scumbag and her not believing me.

I'm guessing now, as an adult, it must have been awful for her to hear this shit because that would mean that maybe she didn't do a background check on her babysitter, but seriously, I still, to this day, don't understand how she could believe some random guy she may have known for a couple of months through her friends, instead of her own daughter. You must sense a glimmer of anger in me here and there, and you would be correct in that vibe. I was deeply and incredibly angry back then.

I don't have too many memories of Bongo other than coming home from school one day and finding my dog Liebe loose on the porch, which never happened. Apparently, our dog pooped again on the rug, and Bongo stepped on it. His shoe size was either twelve or fourteen. That's a lotta cowboy boot in poo. But he put my dog out in the street, Liebe disappeared, and from there, I despised him.

My mom could have simply had a talk with us and said, walk the dog! But she just did whatever her husband told her to do. I came home from school one day, and Liebe was gone for good. He magically disappeared. My mother never explained, and I was to suck it up. To this day, I have never forgotten that. I know a lot of couples get dogs when they're together before kids to kinda test the waters, but my parents got a "family dog," and we had him for at least 8 years. I loved my dog to death, but I was not able to take him out while I was at school, so he pooped on the rug. Apparently, Bongo had enough, and they got rid of him.

There were fights between my mom and Bongo and a lot of stress between my dad and them and us trying to figure this all out. My mom wasn't right in the head. I remember her holding two bottles of booze while she sat crying on the step, telling my brother D and me that she was gonna end it all. We didn't know what to do, so when she left the house, my brother and I took all the booze we could find and dumped it in the sink. She was not happy about that, but hey, we were just kids trying to figure shit out.

The last memory I have of Bongo is of him standing outside of the front of our house with a milk gallon filled with beer. Bongo was a big dude. He was very tall, very big, and had wild, curly, light brown hair. He reminded me of sasquatch. The last day I dealt with him, he was leaning back on his truck, pointing a rifle up to my mom's bedroom window, where we all stood in fear. He was yelling that he was gonna shoot my mom and kill us all after so we wouldn't suffer!! Needless to say, that marriage only lasted six months. They got divorced, and my mom was back on the dating scene.

Eventually, I didn't want to deal with any more shit. I was tired and pretty broken. Now I went through a 2nd divorce. How can you get close to anyone when they all wind up being abusive and leave? At this point in my life, I decided on suicide for the first time. It was not because of Bongo but because I hated everything about my life and this world. I emptied out an entire bottle of aspirin, about ninety pills, and choaked them down in handfuls.

I guess it doesn't seem like a lot, but I was young and weighed about 110 pounds. I went to bed and woke up disappointed to be alive the next morning. I was very sick and lost my hearing. I had a high pitch ringing in my ears piercing through my head, my vision was blurred, I could feel my blood pressure lowering, and my body was not working right, but I knew I had to go to school. About an hour after walking to school, all messed up and out of it, I passed out in the hallway, and my girlfriend Maria got the nurse.

Fifty questions later, I told the nurse that I had tried to kill myself and asked if I could just lie down now. A few hours after, my mom showed up pissed off that she had to leave work for this. She gave me that evil look of nasty and told me I was wasting her time doing this shit and I'd have to stay there and finish out the day because she wasn't taking the day off.

Honestly, I didn't give a shit what she did. I just wanted to hurry up and die. Now the school day is over, and I'm home with my brothers lying on the couch as they play space invaders on Atari, and I get a call from my dad.

Me: Hello

My Dad: yelling at the top of his lungs: "Are you fucking kidding me? You tried to kill yourself, girl. Do you want to die? How bout I come over and kill you myself?"

I was bawling my eyes out, not breathing from the fear of my dad, and quite frankly, exhausted.

My Dad: "Do you understand me, girl, or are we gonna have a problem?"

My Dad never spoke softly. Yelling at the top of his lungs was his specialty. Anyway, miraculously, we all moved on as usual, like nothing ever happened. My mom never said a word to me about any of it. Zero! She came home from work and did her usual. Lay on the couch with a cigarette, a glass of tab, and a newspaper. Sometimes she would treat us to a slice of her pizza if we were lucky or if she was in a good mood.

Weeks went by, and eventually came the one and only Alfonzo, i.e., "Funzy" or "Fungi." I was almost fifteen, he was twenty-five, and my mom was thirty-four. She brought him home one night and introduced him to me. He was definitely different than Bongo but way more twisted. He slowly moved in, and eventually, he followed me around like a dog in heat.

It reminds me of my male cat Boo and how he follows my female cat Buffy around the house with his nose attached to her ass, up and down the steps. I can't stand that, and clearly, Buffy wants nothing to do with that shit either.

I don't think I'll ever fully understand a grown man wanting to be with a teenage girl. It sickens me. But to be honest, it, at the same time, encouraged me to have little faith in men. What is the attraction to a child? So as I got older, I met and knew a lot of men personally who had no problem running their eyes up and down a young girl's body in public. It became a normal thing for me to deal with this behavior, but that didn't mean I appreciated it or enjoyed it. I hated it!

I don't understand watching porn, either, for that matter. It's not that I haven't been exposed to it. Ok, I saw porn for the first time as a child, and the "actors" were pretty old and, quite frankly, gross. Now, if you watch a movie or something on social media, it's humans that are the same age as my kids, doing some pretty F'd up things that are not part of my reality or most others I know, so ya, it makes no sense to me. And I think it takes away any integrity one has left in his body.

Some of the sicker men I know have even bragged about checking out teenage girls to their friends, and when challenged by another man who thought it was sick, they would simply say, "She wants it. Look at her. Look at the way she's dressed. She's asking for it."

I don't know about you, but I know from my own experience and from the mouths of most of my other female friends that young girls don't want old men undressing them in their heads or in real life. We don't want them touching us or considering anything with us. Yeah, sure, there are some females out there that are in trouble emotionally or have Daddy issues who find it easier to latch on to an older guy with some cash. I also know a few young girls who actually love their way older husbands. But honestly, I think it's disturbing and gross, and I can't stand to be around men who think young girls are looking to get raped. That sounds like an excuse for being a predator.

During the time when I was going through my suicide mission, my brother D was dealing with his own demons and introduced me to speed. I really admired my brother D. He was younger than me and protected me as much as he could back then. Nobody at school messed with me anymore once he got into high school. There was a boy that looked at me funny at the water ice store, so my brother beat the daylights out of him. It was awful. My brother had my father's temper and balls of steel. He was just a little boy, but he got into the drug and alcohol scene early.

It was hard not to be in that area where we lived and with all the shit we were trying to deal with. I guess it was the next step for all of us, but either way, we were really close, yet we did our own thing, and we had very different friends.

My brother D came into my room one random night with a bag of speed, crank, or coke, I didn't know the difference back then, but he cut out 2 lines on my end table and told me to try it after he demonstrated how to properly snort with a dollar bill. My brother D, at a very young age, was very intimidating. He reminded me so much of our father with his temper. He could snap in a second and go ballistic and just beat you.

I can't remember how many times he would beat the shit out of me, and it went on here and there for a few years. We were both so angry back then, and I would give up right around the time when I saw my life pass me by. Like wild animals, we fought to the death or until I finally gave in. We haven't spoken in years, but that's a whole other story. He is scary to me still to this day. I remember our little brother S seeing us snort the lines and getting very upset, but we didn't really pay him much mind back then.

It's disturbing, but no one really guided any of us, and S was soo much younger. We were transitioning into teenagers, and though I remember S trying so hard to hang with the big boys, it just didn't happen. If anything, my brother's friends would torture him if he showed up at a party or one of their houses. My guess now is that he really was all alone growing up.

But looking back, I believe it was almost as if I only saw what was meant for me to see. I feel like our relationship is all a blur. I've always felt bad about that, but I didn't know any better back then. We just didn't know how to act. I mean, I thought we ran loose before, but now we were like wild-loose because, at this point, my mom's single, trying to house herself and three kids, working, and probably scared shitless. I would be, for sure.

There was absolutely zero order in our house at this point. By then, I was constantly exposed to drugs, alcohol, and men over double my age that wanted to get into my pants; things little girls should never have to experience, but unfortunately, a lot of us go through this shit, and no one does anything about it.

Alfonzo, Funzy, Fungi, was a wallpaper hanger back when people were obsessed with wallpaper. I think wallpaper was on its way out in the early '80s, and he didn't really work a lot. He was a freeloader, for sure, and my mom had no clue. Or maybe she did, but she clearly would bend over backward for this loser. Funzy was a short, Italian guy with dark brown hair and brown eyes, wearing those old, creepy, gold-frame glasses and a mustache. I thought, at first he was kinda handsome compared to mom's last boyfriend, but it didn't take long for him to show his true colors.

He was always at our house, and in weeks he pretty much moved in, and he was yet another addict. He was one of those alcoholics who turned into a crazy wackjob and hit women and touched little girls when he was drunk, as well as an instigator.

I guess he thought he was smart, but he wasn't. He was extremely nauseating and completely embarrassing to me. The more I think about all of this, the more I feel bad for my mom, but I hated her back then and for a very long time, pretty much most of my life.

Funzy was a scumbag. He would wait for us to get home from school and leave lines of crank on the toilet lid. He would get to my brother first, and as soon as I walked in the door from school, he would tell me, "Suzy, there's something upstairs for you." For the life of me, I guess I was so insecure I would do anything stupid just to fit in. I would literally be like, "Oh, ok, thanks," not really getting that he had other plans for me and consciously scoped everything out. Get my brother hooked, get me involved so I would feel guilty or indebted to him for something, and then go in for the kill.

He was a predator. He probably figured neither one of us would say anything since we were using the stuff he left for us, and back then, we didn't. We were just as guilty as him in his mind. But then he took it to another level. One night I found a vial of cocaine in my mom's handbag while searching for a dollar. She was doing this shit too. He had us all trapped in his web.

He used to send my mom out to get him a six-pack of beer even though he had a big bottle of crown royal cracked open and half empty. She would do anything for this guy. Even if she just walked in the door from a long day at work, she would stop everything and go get him his beer. I know I was just a teenager then, but I knew that this guy wasn't contributing to our household or helping my mother in any way, and she still kept him around.

Once she left the house, within seconds, he would get close to my face and start talking to me like a weirdo. If I was in the kitchen, he'd start calling me "Suzy" - "Suzy" like a bird that couldn't sing, then he would push his body up against mine and back me into the refrigerator door and try to make out with me while gripping my wrists above my head. It was sickening, he would slur and breathe heavily, and his hot breath stunk of booze. I was afraid, and I was utterly disgusted at the same time. Disgusted with my mother and the fact that she had zero instinct whatsoever and would bring a stranger into her home with her three young children.

It disgusted me that I had to endure this abuse, twisting and turning my neck while trying to avoid her dirtball boyfriend's tongue sliding into my mouth forcefully. I was pretty much disgusted with everything about him and my mother at that point, but I stayed silent.

If I was upstairs and my mom was at work, he would come into my room naked. I would yell at him, "Get the fuck out," and tell him he was disgusting. I tried not to make too much about it, so he would just leave, and sometimes he would, but not without a speech about what's natural, like being naked. He and my mom had planned a week-long getaway, and before they left, he asked me to come into the bedroom because he had something to tell me.

He made me sit on the bed next to him and then proceeded to tell me that he was not in love with my mom and wished that he and I were going away instead. I was fifteen! He would undress in front of me and ask me why I was so uncomfortable.

"God made us this way. We weren't born with clothes Suzy."

Oh, ok, my bad, what an asshole. It was all I could do to get away from him, praying he wouldn't try to rape me. This was all the fucking time, and I couldn't tell my mom because she didn't speak to me other than making lists of what I had to do every day after school. I know she felt it, but I guess she was in denial.

Funzy would just stare at me and tell me I looked pretty, and my mom would just make a stink face. If looks could kill, I would have been gone years ago. So I would get out of that house when he was there as much as possible. I remember my first frosh hop with this cute guy Andrew I met at the skating rink. He came to my house, and Funzy let him in while I was getting ready upstairs. My mom had just left to grab some beer.

The whole time Andrew waited there, I could hear Funzy downstairs drunk, singing, well it was more like howling really, "Andy, Andy, boy." I wanted to die. There I was, stressing as I put on my mom's adult blue polyester dress and her shoes because she didn't have the money to buy me a dress, embarrassed, and mortified as her drunk boyfriend was making fun of my date. After that night, I never heard from Andrew again.

There was a time when Funzy was so sloshed he and my mom were yelling back and forth, he was breaking shit, and I was pretty much done. I just didn't have the energy to care anymore. She ordered me to clean the kitchen, and I got pissed off because I was tired of being their personal slave. I get that chores are fair, but I was literally ordered with a list to clean the entire house every day after school, clean the kitchen and dishes every night and do everyone's wash. Her last husband's wash, her wash, and both my brother's wash.

She would even call me after school and offer me $5.00 if I would do extra and clean her bedroom because she had company that night. But if I asked her to help me with homework, she would say, "You have a set of encyclopedias. I'm not doing your work for you, girl. Look it up."

I told her I hated her and her piece of a shit drunk boyfriend. She defended him, of course, took a hi-healed shoe, and hit me in the face with it. The shoe ripped my earring out and put a nice scar on my face under my left eye.

I decided to call my dad, praying that he would save us. I told him as quickly as I could what was going on. My Dad knew nothing as we were ordered to keep our mouths shut. I told him that Funzy was drunk all the time and that he was trying to touch me, and that he was giving us drugs. My mom grabbed me and started hitting me while he was on the call, then took the phone and hung it up.

I was immediately ordered to go to my room. After that, I heard the phone calls, I heard the panic in my mother's voice, and I heard Funman run to call his wallpaper boss Alan. This guy was another piece of shit of a human. A while back, I met Funzy's boss and was asked to babysit his daughter.

Funzy took me over to Alan's house one day to discuss a job he had, and Alan was telling him that I was a nice piece of ass. OMG, I could hear them, and I was afraid. I could also see from their body language that I should be afraid. Alan was another short, fat, hairless dirtbag who liked little girls. I got this sick feeling in the pit of my gut and tried to wander into another room, looking for an escape door in case I was going to get gang raped.

He was nudging Funzy to get with me. UGH, I hated that they could just do that shit and get away with it. By the way, thank God I never babysat for Alan, and thank God Funzy had a glimmer of humanity that day and chose to leave when he did!

About an hour later that same night, we had company. My Dad was on his way, and Alan showed up as well. Now all four adults were in the living room arguing, and my dad really didn't know what was going on. He only knew what I said in the two-second phone call. The Parents called me downstairs, and my dad asked me what had happened in front of everyone. So I vomited it all, even about the boss telling Funman that I was a hot piece of ass.

Just a reminder again, I was fifteen, Funzy was twenty-five, his boss was at least forty-five, bald, fat, and creepy, and my mom was thirty-four. All three on the wrong side stood up, arguing that I was not right in the head. To them, I was obviously lying.

"We don't know why she would make something like this up."

My Dad was furious and obviously confused. My mom grabbed me in front of them all, dragged me to the front door by my hair, and whispered in my ear with her hot breath and spit,

"What are you trying to do to me girl? Are you trying to ruin my life?"

It was over in a flash, and my dad left.

The three of them convinced my dad that I had made all of this up, and he believed them. I still don't understand why he believed them. I wonder if maybe he just didn't know what to do or if maybe he couldn't handle the situation, but it was hard to see him walk out as I was left upstairs as the mental patient. Here I had this image of this angry, strong man, my father, that could probably beat the shit out of those two knuckleheads in a few minutes, but other than drive there and back home, he did nothing.

I don't know; maybe he's only good at beating little kids and women. But in my gut, I believe that my mom told him a story about me on the down low. Maybe, she told him that I was always giving her a hard time or something like that to try and save her own ass. Can you sense here that I had a bit of an edge attached to me?

Blows my mind how a parent could be so disconnected to the point where their own child's words mean nothing to them. I wonder what my mother was thinking. Did she think I made all of this up just to start trouble? Why would I, and what would I have to gain? I think she was worried that she would lose that dick face of a boyfriend and be alone. She would have to start all over again, and who wants to do that after putting a few months into all of this drama?

Sarcasm is something I acquired from my mom.

It wasn't like we were going to be closer if I forced her to be all alone with her kids. I wanted to see her happy. I can break this all down now and have a clearer picture of her mindset, but I still can't understand choosing a man over your child.

A few weeks after that, Funzy was hammered and beat my mom again. She was making a pot of spaghetti sauce, a really big pot. One of those pots you could fit a twenty-pound roast in, and Funzy was wasted! He started pushing her around in the kitchen, and then he became violent.

"I know this is awful, but I always thought he was a little pussy. I would watch my dad in action, and let me assure you, we were frightened to the core. When Funzy let loose, I would just think to myself, "OMG, here we go, another long night of BS." That's how wired for the trauma I was. All I could think about was how late we would be up this night, how soon I had to get up for school, and whether or not the cops would show up again.

Funzy took the whole pot of red sauce and threw it up against the wall. Sauce everywhere! I ran into the kitchen to stop them, and my mom told me to call 911. Back then, we didn't have cell phones in our hands. We had to run to the nearest rotary phone plugged into a wall.

I ran; Funzy chased me, grabbed me, and threw me into the glass table headfirst. I was out for the count! I didn't know if I was unconscious because I had a lot of out-of-body experiences as a kid, but I can remember that even though my body felt paralyzed and I couldn't move, I could still see with my eyes closed and hear everything clearly. I was outside my body. Oddly enough, my mother was holding and rocking me, crying. She moaned, "what did you do," and Funzy was scared.

Amazingly and all of a sudden, they both seemed to have souls in their otherwise selfish and cold meat-suits. But it was all an act because the deep question of the night was probably, "how was this going to look?" Especially since this was only days after the big meeting when my mom sent my dad home.

Well, my being knocked out by my mom's drunk boyfriend slowed things down a bit, but not for long. Eventually, my brother D was at the front door, so Funzy panicked and locked it. D went around back to the basement, and Funzy grabbed a bat and ran down to lock that door. I snapped out of it. I was aware at that point that this jerk-off had a bat and my brother was in danger, so I got up, opened the front door, and ran outside.

Before you know it, the four of us are out front now, and once again, Funzy goes after my mom, this time ripping her shirt, so D beat his ass on the front lawn. Our friends and some neighbors joined in breaking things up, and my brother D and Fungi man were both locked up that night.

Our house was at the top of the street on the corner. We were the house that always had cop cars in front of it. It was made of big, silver-looking stones. Great for climbing as I frequently lost my house keys. At night in the spring and summer, you could see hundreds of big black water bugs crawling on the front and sides. Beds of shiny back, black bugs on the grass like a carpet. I never saw so many water bugs in my life.

CHAPTER 09 | SHE'S A LITTLE RUNAWAY

There was always some kind of crazy screaming and fighting going on in our house. That night after my brother and Fucknuts, sorry, Funzy, got arrested, I left home and walked away barefoot in my pajamas. I walked from Upper Darby, Pennsylvania, through Yeadon, Pennsylvania, and wound up somewhere in West Philadelphia, and it was not good. My destination was my good grandparent's house in Southwest Philly, I believe fourteen miles away.

It was dark out, and the rain started to pour down. I was by myself in my jammies, walking in a neighborhood unknown to me. I started noticing that there were strange people, probably hookers and gangs, on every corner and graffiti on every building.

It's funny now, not funny, haha, but at the time, I thought I was smart, so I picked up a big tree branch in case I had to defend myself. I was lucky to be alive that night. All I wanted to do was get to my memom's house. Memom was my mother's mother, my other grandmother.

She was my "grandmom goodie, " the kind one, the loveable grandmom, at least to me. Memom was tiny, maybe four foot two, with short white hair. She used to waddle when she walked. She was so cute to me. My dad used to call her Fuzz. I guess because her hair was so fuzzy. And my grandfather was handsome, with green eyes and brown hair. She and my grandfather were like The Parents I never had. They never disciplined me, but they loved me and let me stay there.

MEMOM

I lived with them off and on for a long time. I guess they knew what was going on even though nobody ever spoke about it at their house. I had two completely different sets of grandparents. They couldn't have been any more different. I miss my memom and grandpop terribly sometimes, and thirty years later, I still remember their phone number, 492-0193. They were always good to me.

I was walking in the middle of the night, in the rain, in my jammies with a big stick, by myself, scared shitless, and barefoot. I had no idea where my grandparent's house was, but I knew I was close. At one point, a man, maybe in his early 20s, came up to me and asked me what I was doing in that neighborhood. I got scared, but he told me he wanted to help, so I just asked him how to get to Southwest Philly or to the trolly.

Back then, we took trolleys and buses or walked when we wanted to go somewhere. So I kinda thought that if I found a bus or trolley, I could ask the driver if he knew how to get to my Memom's address. I know, I know, but I was still a child. Anyway, the guy walked me to the corner where the trolley would stop. I thanked him, and he left.

While waiting for a trolley, I realize that I have no pockets, no shoes, and soaking wet with no change for the ride. And here come the trolls. A man comes up to me in an officer's uniform and asks me if I'm ok. I thought it was pretty obvious that I had been hysterical for a few good hours, drenched and in my pj's with no shoes. So, my sarcasm and ego blinded my instincts. He asked me where I was going, and I told him, "I'm trying to find my grandparent's house, but I'm lost, and I don't have any change for the trolley."

I guess I was simply hoping that he would give me some change and call it a day, but instead, he said, "don't worry, come with me. See that church across the street with the fence around it? I work there. You can go there and call your grandparents and get dried off."

At this point, I was worn out, so I went to the church with him. I guess I figured we were going to a church so what could possibly go wrong? Maybe I should have pondered on that one a little longer. We get inside, and he immediately locks the top bolt. Of course, then, in my head, I was saying to myself, "Great, here we go, another dirtbag."

I really didn't have too much feeling inside me anymore. It was like I was just numb to everything. He sat down and told me to relax and that everything was going to be ok.

"Damn, I just wanted to use the phone, but he wouldn't stop talking. "

I'm so worn out that in my mind, he's a cop, but then I realize he was merely a security guard. He was about six feet tall, very dark-skinned with glasses, a mustache, and in uniform. He wasn't mean or aggressive. In fact, it seemed like he had a good bone in his body. But I couldn't have been more wrong. He was slowly going to the dark side with me. He started asking me questions about what had happened and how did I get to this area. I was crying and telling him all my personal shit, etcetera, etcetera, just unloading. I know better now not to elaborate on my private stuff to anyone, but I was young and pretty dumb, just begging for someone to listen to me.

I suppose for a second, it felt good to think that someone actually cared, but a second later, I realized that he didn't. He started talking to me about the demons that were inside my body and, of course, that he worked at this church and could perform an exorcism on me. And obviously, these demons were the reason I was experiencing all of that trauma and evil.

Now, that was not the first time I had people tell me that they needed to perform and exorcism on me. In fact, it was happening for me the third time because I made the mistake of telling people about my out-of-body experiences, seeing dead people, and my issues at home. So, the analysis and consensus were that this was a byproduct of all the demons that surrounded me. Clearly, this guy was a security guard, not a priest, and now I'm really scared.

He changed the subject for a minute and said, "How bout we get you out of those wet clothes? I have a whole room full of clothes that were donated to the church downstairs. Come on, follow me."

And so, the next segment of my nightmare began...

I followed him through dark hallways and up and down long staircases. It was like I was trapped in a complicated maze, and I watched myself, almost out of my body, wondering what was coming next and afraid. It was so dark I couldn't see much of anything. Down the steps we go, and into another room full of boxes and clothes. I could smell mildew in the air and feel the dampness from the pouring rain all around me. I tried to memorize the maze we walked through, but there was barely any light to see clearly.

He told me to pick anything I wanted to wear and closed the door, then opened the door, then closed the door. This went on for a few minutes and was incredibly annoying to me. After a while, I lost my patience and said, "I'm good, thanks." I took a pass on changing into dry donated clothes because I knew I was in trouble here.

Again, I can't imagine the mindset or thought process of a grown-ass man wanting to watch a little girl undress. He seemed fine and told me to follow him again down another long hallway in the darkness. At this point, we're in the back of the church. As I was walking, I lost my vision of him as if he had disappeared in front of me. To the right of me, I could feel and see an entire wardrobe of Priest's robes hanging up and rubbing across my arm.

Out of the silence, I hear, "are you a virgin?" It was so random, and his voice echoed through the big, opened, dark church, and I thought, 'what the heck man, why is this happening?' I was at a loss for words, but I said, "Um, I gotta go. I have a boyfriend."

At that point, we were literally in the middle of the church in the dark. I could see the pews and Jesus hanging on the cross above my head. I'd never been on that side of a church and didn't ever wish to be again. I told him I had to go to the bathroom, so we went back upstairs as he went on and on about performing this exorcism on me. It felt like I had walked through the longest maze in the world and like I was there for hours. I was so scared and stressed out.

We made it upstairs, and he took a phone call. I sat there listening to his hum-drum conversation, and immediately, my eyes connected with the entrance door. I gathered that he wasn't in a rush to rape me, so I found the right moment, got up quickly, and unlocked the door. I bolted, as fast as I could, across the church parking lot. It was still dark and still raining, so I took a wild guess about my direction. I was running and running, never looking back until, eventually, I could tell by the houses around me that I was close to my grandparents.

The sun was just coming up, the birds were chirping, and I was still lost. As I was feeling a little safer and half dead, I noticed these two guys moving furniture out of one of the row homes.

The one guy yells across the street, asking if I'm ok. At this point, I was completely out of my mind and just frightened by anyone who even looked at me. He asked again, and I said, "I'm good, thank you."

He was a young and handsome guy, roughly in his early twenties. He tried to talk to me, and somehow, I sensed he was a good human being. So I asked him, "Do you know where Guyer Avenue is? I'm trying to get to my grandparent's house." I continued telling him that I ran away last night, and this and that and blah, blah, happened.

I wish I could find this guy today and just thank him for being so kind to me and for being a good person. He told me his grandmom died and left him her house, and he really didn't know the area, but I could come in and get some water and food. Of course, I was hesitant, but I had to go to the bathroom, and I was exhausted and hungry, so I went in.

He gave me water and made me a peanut butter sandwich. He gave me a pair of jeans and a hoodie and let me get changed upstairs. Then, he sat with me, and we talked about music. He was going to an Ozzie Ozborne concert that night, which I thought was really cool, and all of a sudden, I remembered that I had just auditioned a few weeks prior to this drama for a new TV show called Dancin' on Air and was waiting to see if I made the cut or not. Which I later found out that I did.

How funny is that? I just went through all this drama and trauma, and in an instant, even in my exhaustion, I still found a way to think about something cool in my life. He told me he would be there for a while, and if I felt safe enough, I could go upstairs and sleep for a little with the door locked, so I did for maybe an hour. But my mind was racing, and I couldn't really sleep because I was on a mission to find my grandparent's house.

Eventually, I got up and thanked him for his kindness, but I had to find my grandparent's house, so I left and started walking. The sun was up, and for the first time in the past few hours, I felt safe. This sounds crazy, but the one thing I always remember about my grandparent's house was waking up to the sound of the birds chirping. I loved that, and to this day, I still feel like the birds are up early in the morning hanging out, having tea parties, and conversing.

And while I was walking, that's all I could hear, and somehow, in my short time, I found a sense of peace, and then I found their house. My grandfather hugged me when he opened the door, and he asked me if I was ok. I was slightly embarrassed but too weak to get into the conversation, but also relieved to see my grandfather's face. I went upstairs to my favorite tiny bedroom at the top of the hall and passed out.

I could hear the phone calls that my Memom was making to let everyone know I was ok and that I was there, and eventually, my mom showed up.

I knew it was inevitable that my mom would show up, but she was the last person I wanted to see. She sat on the side of my bed and woke me up, saying she was so sorry, and she was so worried. I didn't believe her. I believed she looked like a shitty mom and wanted to change that view. Unfortunately, I had to go back home at that time.

Everything was different that week. My mom was the perfect mom. She sat down and, for the first time in my life, had a conversation with me. She asked me if I was the one who cut Funzy's brake lines because his Bronco was fine until the day after the last episode at our house. She said that they almost couldn't stop coming to a light one day. It's interesting that she picked that particular topic at the time, as I thought it was kinda random, but I suppose she was trying to put the pieces together.

I had some friends who knew what was going on in our house. Well, most of the neighborhood knew, but a couple of my friends offered to cut his brake lines, and even though I didn't fully understand what that meant at the time, I just wanted him out of our lives, so I said yes. Now at fifty-five, I would never even consider something like that, but at fifteen, my mind was not altogether, and I just wanted a normal, happy life. I couldn't process the consequences or what was really going on.

My mom starts winning my trust again by talking to me, which she never would normally do, and I tell her all the shit that Funzy did to me. I told her everything, every detail. I told her that I wasn't lying about her friend Rutt either. She seemed to believe me. She got very angry and promised me that I would never have to go through anything like that again. She would never bring Funzy into our house again, and on top of that, she would have his legs broken.

Back then, you could get away with shit like that. Obviously, things have changed over the years. But no one ever touched Funzy.

She made me promise not to tell my father or my brothers because it would just make the situation so much worse, so I never spoke a word of it. I'm guessing my brother D would have killed Funzy anyway if he knew. The conversation is over, and I go into my room as if nothing ever happened and start living again. I took a deep breath and felt comfort in that conversation because I believed her. Just like that, I recovered and let it all go because, for some reason, I believed my mom, and the resistance and anger were gone. But it didn't take long for her to go back on her word.

A couple of days later, I was in my room singing as I did every day for hours with my bedroom door closed and music blasting. My mom came into my room in a rush and said, "We have a guest coming over today. I want you to be nice." A dreadful phrase she used often that haunted me. I knew in an instant who that guest was, and my heart started racing, my body started shaking, and I lost my mind. I said, "Are you kidding me? You're bringing that drunk into our house after everything I told you he did?" She told me he was away long enough and got sober, so everything will be different now. Sober in seven days, that's amazing!

Apparently, my brother D found this info out as well. I'll never forget him coming into my bedroom with big green trash bags ordering me to pack my shit. I knew what he meant and started emptying my clothes frantically into the bags. At the time, D had a cast on his hand and wrist. He said he fell down the hill at school a week prior, but I always wondered if he tried to hurt himself and failed.

We tied ropes to the bags and shimmied them down from my bedroom window to the sidewalk. I had no idea where we were going, and neither did D. We just knew we were done.

I remember yelling out my bedroom window to my friends across the street, telling them Funzy's back, and before I could get to the bottom of the stairs, two of my friends came into my house and went into the kitchen where Funman and Mom were having coffee as if nothing ever happened and as if life was so great and normal. I wonder where I can buy that mindset.

My friends proceeded to tell my mom that she was a piece of shit for choosing this scumbag over her own kids. She immediately ordered them out of the house. D was already out ahead of me, and I uncomfortably followed behind my friends. My Mom held the screen door open as I walked out, tilting her head dramatically left and right as she squawked, "poor, poor Suzy didn't get her way again."

I wanted to punch her in the face, but I was too afraid, and of course, I could never do something like that. I just cried and walked away, meeting up with D to grab our bags and go anywhere but here. We had nowhere to go, we tried to get a ride to our dad's house, but that wasn't happening. We stayed out for a few nights since the weather was nice and eventually just came back. Honestly, it was not a big deal for us to sleep on a bench outside or in someone's basement. Sometimes, you just do what you gotta do.

Not too long after, Funzy tried talking to me when no one was around. He acted like I was crazy and said that he had never touched me, nor would he ever consider doing so. What a

narcissist! I became a hardcore walking zombie at that point.
I just responded OK, OK, yeah, OK, and did what I had to do
to get through each day until I could figure something out.

The fucked-up thing is that everyone knew something was
going on, but nobody did anything. This baffled me as
everyone I knew in my family talked so much shit and knew
everyone's business, but when it came down to it, nobody did
a fucking thing to help us. Everyone had a big mouth. My mom
used to say that the ones that talk the most do the least. She
was right about that.

CHAPTER 10 | SATINSKY INSTITUTE

A few days or so later, I told my mother I couldn't deal with her or her boyfriend. I hated being there and did not want to live with her anymore. I added that I hated school and wanted to quit. I had already failed 11th grade and had to repeat it. I just couldn't imagine another two years of high school or living there anymore. I told my mother I needed therapy. I needed help now! I had been through too much. I told her that there was a place that I could go to that accepted health insurance for payment.

I knew my dad had health insurance because it was an ongoing fight between my mother and him. One of my girlfriends left our High School and went to this school in the city, Satinsky Institute for human research and development. I remember it being a place where you could graduate high school, prep and generate college credits, and have therapy every day.

One-on-one therapy, art therapy, family therapy, group therapy, etc. Therapy was mandatory, but classes were not. I had to have an evaluation first to qualify. Much to my surprise, my mom broke down and made the appointment. We took a train to the city. To get into this school, you had to go through a bank on the corner of third street in Philly and take an elevator to one of the top floors. When we walked in, there were hallways and doors everywhere. The classrooms looked like the same classrooms in my school but with tall windows overlooking the city.

It was time, and there we sat with Dr. Satinsky a week later. Dr. Satinsky kind of looked like his name suggests. He was an older guy with white hair and glasses, and he wore a long white medical jacket. He asked me a ton of questions pertaining to why I thought I needed to be there.

I remember the entire interview basically telling him I wanted to die and all the reasons behind that statement. My mother was mortified. I guess she thought I was going to sit in silence, I really don't know, but I told him as much as I could because I felt safe there. She kept saying at the interview that I was creating drama, I was lying, and there was nothing wrong with me until Dr. Satinsky nicely asked her to shut up, and then he told her that she was the problem.

I wound up getting accepted into that school. A few days later, my mom called me from work and told me it was fine if I quit high school and went to Satinsky Institute.

I guess she figured she really didn't have a choice, and my only other options were to live with my memom or be on the streets. Or maybe she thought it would be easier for her to live her life without me getting in her way. At least she wouldn't have to worry about her boyfriend drooling over her teenage daughter. Who knows for sure? I was happy about that phone call.

I started taking the train to the city every day. I felt like I was finally free. I went to this new school with new faces, all different colors, shapes, sizes, and rich kids with deep emotional issues. My sense was that most of them had parents who didn't want to deal with them at all. They all seemed lonely, insecure, and quiet. Some were loud in the way they dressed or in the amount of ink and pins on their bodies. One big guy had a tik where he would snort mucus and twitch his neck randomly. That was tuff to deal with during art therapy when everyone was aligned quietly creating. I was gagging.

One girl had a tall, bright red, very stiff mohawk that stood straight up at least six inches, the sides of her head were completely shaved, and she had many pins in her ears and face. She was quiet, I never heard her speak, but I could feel the pain in her.

My girlfriend Marie and I would get invited to their houses in the city to party during lunch. Some of the houses were incredible. The décor inside was rich and really over-the-top fancy compared to where I was living. I always wondered what their parents were like and what they did for a living because it is not cheap to live in the city!

There were all kinds there, so I fit in easily, but this environment was a lot different. It was all on me to figure my shit out with no one to guide me, which shouldn't have made a difference either way, but it was a bit unsettling. Now I had to be responsible for taking classes, and I didn't want to. I just wanted therapy. I really enjoyed and learned a lot from group, art and one-on-one therapy.

Once a week, I believe every Thursday was family therapy, and guess who never showed up? My family just couldn't make it. So how do you fix the root of the problem when the roots are pretending to be the flower? You don't. I pretended that one of them, at the very least, would show up, but they never did, so I just worked on fixing myself without them.

I felt even more alone than ever. A few weeks in, I met this older guy Harris who was about thirty-five years old and owned a hotdog cart outside of the school. He had a standard, small metal hotdog cart with chips, cookies, soda, and sausage sandwiches. I would come out of the bank entrance for lunch and grab a hotdog and chips.

Harris was Greek and had a heavy accent. He was short, fat, and balding with black hair and brown eyes, and he was very hairy. Humm, sounds familiar. He asked a lot of questions when I stopped by. He seemed like a nice guy, but I knew something was off. I couldn't trust my gut anymore because I didn't trust anything, so when I would get that pull inside or that red flag, I'd ignore it because I felt that pull all the time. It was 24-7 survivor mode for me.

I told him I was a singer and that I was going to get discovered one day and make it big. God, I sound so dumb right now, but I really believed it. He tells me he knows major producers and can help me. Then followed up by asking me to work for him after school cleaning his carts and restocking them.

Well, of course, this guy knows producers that can help me, so I'm going to work for him, right? And no doubt I needed the money.

After a few weeks, he started telling me he must take me to meetings in NY to sit with these big-time producers, so he bought me dresses and shoes to wear with the budget money the producers gave him because I had nothing like that in my closet. This goes on for a little while, and he just takes me to dinner meetings and makes up stories as to why no one else showed up. He did pull some strings, and I got to eat dinner with Connie Stevens who I was supposed to sing with that night, which never happened. I didn't even know who she was. We had like ten minutes with her then she left.

That was awkward and should be very telling for anyone who had a clue. Not me, of course. You could tell me the sky was green, and I'd figure out a way to believe you as I looked at the blue sky. Harris wants me to come over to his house. Well, it was his mother's house. I remember the anger behind the face she gave me when I walked in, but I didn't pay her any mind because Harris told me she was his sister and to ignore her. She was scary, and they communicated in Greek. After a couple of years of hanging out with a lot of Greeks in my new neighborhood, I picked up some of the language and could understand without speaking to them.

I was pretty good at translating tones and body language. After a minute or so, sister-mom left the room. It was all so shady, and only a young, naive teenager would fall for this crap, and I did.

I think I would have done anything to get away from my life. At the time, I had my first real boyfriend, George, and working with Harris was taking time away from my relationship. George and I were young, and we were in puppy love. He was always there for me when shit went down with my mom. He was friends with my brother and with all of my other friends, and he was a good guy, but I was so worried about losing this opportunity to get signed by a record label that I spent all my time practicing and going to no-show meetings.

Weeks go by, and I thought I was building a friendship with Harris. He would ask me about my family, and I would tell him what was going on. At one point, he told me he was in the

Greek mob and that he would take care of my mother's boyfriend if I wanted him to. So I considered it but left it on the back burner. Eventually, Harris started telling me that the producers wanted me to sign a contract, and he had to be my manager because he did all of the leg work. If you saw this contract, you would either die laughing at how pathetic it was or just feel sorry for me because I was clearly disconnected and hypnotized in the opposite direction of reality.

I believe I still have that contract somewhere in my mountains of storage of "the things I could never let go of," but either way, this "contract" was one page, written by someone who literally couldn't speak English or spell. It was a joke. Basically, he owned me for 10 years, but I didn't understand this. I decided to tell my mom, and to my surprise, she stepped up and took me to an entertainment lawyer. The one good thing I can say about my mom is that she never stopped me from singing. Occasionally, she would ask me to turn the music down, but for the most part, she seemed to support my practicing every day in my bedroom. You'll find out why in the end.

The lawyer flat-out explains to me that "This is shit." I cried. I blamed my mom and told her she was always trying to ruin my life, something she would tell me a lot, and we left. I actually feel sort of bad now for making her feel bad after she tried to do something nice for me, but I had reached the point of no return with her back then.

Of course, when I tell Harris this, he starts making fake phone calls and talks in Greek, and now I can't understand a thing he's saying. From there, the new deal is that I must start rehearsing at Harris's parent's house in his unfinished basement with a cassette player. There was a rotary payphone on the wall, and every once in a while, it would ring, and Harris would tell me it was the producers checking to make sure I was there. I wouldn't be surprised if I found out he had people calling just to make it all seem legit.

One night at "rehearsal," Harris starts shmoozzing me, so now I'm confused because he has never made advances at me before, and after all, I'm only sixteen now, and he's thirty-five so why would he, and oohhh, Suzanne, why are you suddenly surprised? Yes, you guessed it, here we go again, another dirtbag.

That night started out normal even though there was nothing normal about any of this. Harris started to work his way into my space. My guess is that he started to panic, or maybe he felt that he had put so much time and energy into manipulating me that he had to take it to the next level. I mean, clearly, he took some time trying to write up a legal document that he thought sounded legit. He bought me a few dresses for these fake meetings and gave me a job cleaning and restocking his hotdog cart, so I guess I owed him something, right?

But as a thirty-five-year-old man, what is your level of thinking in this situation with a teenage girl? Where does the twist in your brain start when you truly believe that, somehow, this little girl is what you want or that she owes you something?

Harris came closer, grabbed my shoulders, and proceeded to pull me into his space. He forcefully pushed me to the floor and held my body down. I was struggling quietly, not sure why I was so quiet, but I guess fear took over. He tried to kiss me, I fought and said no, but he was not having any of that. It was only minutes, yet it seemed like a lifetime. Everything was dragging out in slow motion. Even the sound was muffled in my head. I hate this feeling. My body was shutting down.

Eventually, Harris rapes me on the dirty, cold, cement basement floor. I'll never forget how sick I was. His fat, hairy body was on top of me, holding me down, and he had major BO! I could hear my elbows, my tailbone, and my skull scraping against the cement floor. I could feel my back and exposed skin bleeding and my hair coming out of my head as he held me down forcefully.

He was disgusting, and I went into shock. I was out of my body once again. I remember shutting down completely and watching this entire scene from above myself. Like a scene in the movies when someone dies on the hospital bed and comes out of their body, then goes back in fully aware of what just happened yet feeling nothing but love. The difference was that I couldn't feel anymore. I couldn't hear anything except his heavy breathing, and I prayed that I was finally dead. I think my guides or God or a spirit of protection came in to save me from feeling all of that.

When he was done, he got up off me and acted like nothing ever happened. Just walked away, mumbling something under his breath. I laid there on the cement floor for a while, then got up and tried to put myself back together. I walked out and walked home that night with a completely different personality. I had no fear anymore, and I didn't care about anything. I didn't even cry. I had been through a lot of shit, but this was beyond anything I could grasp, and as usual, I couldn't tell anyone.

After that, I stopped going to Satinsky. I stopped speaking to Harris and fell into a deep depression. I draw a blank on some things from my past. I forgot more than I could remember, as the ancestors would say.

I didn't remember the rape until I was back in therapy when I was twenty. I had completely blocked it out until I started this specific therapy called EMDR, Eye movement desensitization and reprocessing therapy, which brought up way too many horrible memories at once. EMDR is a mental health treatment technique. It involves moving your eyes a specific way by following a small Ping-Pong-like ball on a screen as it bounces left and right. I also had pulse tabs on my fingers to feel the vibration of each bounce and headphones to hear beeps with each bounce.

The goal is to help you heal from trauma or other distressing life experiences by recognizing each event and purposefully placing them into a separate imaginary box and, for me, storing them on a big imaginary bookshelf until I was ready to face and process each event one at a time. EMDR was probably the best therapeutic experience for me at that time, yet at the same time, it was agonizing to relive everything I had unknowingly buried deep inside me.

When I remembered this incident, I shut down for months once again. My doctor prescribed a stronger dose of anti-depressants and Xanax for anxiety.

I wish that I had known back then what I know now and worked on these issues another way. For me, therapy was good and very necessary, but after a while, I realized that all we did was talk about the traumas. I wasn't given any methods or practices on how to heal them. I never told my boyfriend about the rape, but by that time, he was with another girl, and we remained friends for a while after.

Eventually, things stirred up again with Funzy and Mom, so I called Harris to see if he could help my brother and me get a ride to my dad's house in New Jersey. Sad, isn't it? This guy raped me, and I still went back to ask for help because he was the only person I knew with a car that wouldn't try and stop me or tell my mother my plan. I had no one that could help me except for my rapist. I guess sometimes you do what you gotta do, and we made it to New Jersey to try and get help from our father.

I couldn't tell my father everything because I was so afraid of him, and D didn't have the same story as I did. And for some reason, we both wanted to protect our mom., so we left out a lot of the details and just said that we couldn't live there anymore.

In 1984, at the ripe young age of 17, I decided it was time to be a big girl and join a real band. I was staying with my father and his girlfriend Diana, who I earlier address as my stepmother. One day I picked up and started reading a magazine called the musician's grapevine. Whoa, I remembered hearing about this magazine a while back in Upper Darby hanging out with older musicians.

I can find a band here! Long story short, I auditioned for an original band and got the job. This is where I met my best friend back then, Gary. He ran the show, wrote the music and lyrics, and was the lead guitar player. He was my mentor and taught me more about life than anyone I've ever met. He saved me many times from ending it all and was always there to help me out whenever I was going down a bad path.

I really was blessed from the start to have met him and to always have a great bunch of guys in my band who could play their instruments like mofos! They were all brothers to me, and over time we all became extremely close. We even rented a big old shack in Clementon, New Jersey, 58 Elm Street. What a shit hole! Most of us had day jobs, but we would be up all-night jamming. It was probably the best time of my life, with great memories, hours and hours of group talks, rehearsals, and laughs.

It would take me years to write out all of the adventures we had, the photo shoots, dance instructors, and strippers auditioning to be part of our show. That was Gary's idea. A two-for-one deal. Hire strippers and get laid. Or at least try to, haha. Gary and his business mind... But in all honesty, I can say that my guys in our band Midnight Angel were rated PG compared to the cover scene and the things that would go on backstage with random women and married ass men.

Gary, Brett, Me, Pat, and Dave

Original bands didn't play much, and you always worked for free until you built up a following. Back then, in the 80s, there were a lot of "hair bands," and to be honest, I loved it. I loved every second of being in a band. I sucked at first for a while, but Gary thought I had a shot. Those were my most insecure times. I knew I could sing; my mirror knew I could sing, and my hairbrush knew I could sing, but to sing in a real band, on stage in front of people, was my biggest fear. After all, the only time I sang in front of anyone was in a school talent show and an Al Albert's audition, all before I was fourteen.

I was so afraid of what everyone would say because I never had anyone really support my singing or tell me I was any good, for that matter. I only knew that I was a skinny, redheaded, freckled-faced, bucked-toothed, ugly beaver because that was what I was told most of my life growing up by my brother and kids from school.

Gary tried to manage my situation but fumbled when his brain gave him the great idea to use reverse psychology on me and verbally abuse me. The "C word" was one of his favs. I despised that word like most women, and everything he said would backfire on him. I wound up leaving a few times but always came back. Like a stray dog, I always come back. Obviously, he had no idea how broken I was from seventeen + years of abuse, but Gary was a good soul and a very generous human and still is today. He just didn't know how to handle me back then, and he most certainly had his own demons to deal with.

Gary would yell at me all the time when I wasn't loud enough or if I sounded lame. He wanted me to be a natural star on stage, but I would stand there paralyzed, finding my attention on my bottom lip and right leg as they both shook in unison throughout the entire gig. I can remember smelling the dryer sheet scent on my clothing and pondering on it in a daze while up on stage.

I felt like I was trapped in a bad dream, and the spotlight was on me, so everyone could see my issues and how ugly I was. I felt like every female there hated me because, in my mind, they stared at me and made fun of me, just like in school and just as my mother did. But I became better with time. Not fast enough for Gary, so he paid one of his old singers Deveraux, to teach me how to relax and find a niche, my own sound or voice hook to make me stand out from the rest, but I only wound-up mimicking stupid sex sounds in my verses like Madonna. Ugh, not my deal at all, but I tried. And unfortunately, it's all recorded.

I used to cringe when I listened to that cassette, "Live from Fantasy Theater, Midnight Angel." Now I imagine that voice to be one of my children and find pride in it.

Gary (blonde, on the right) was crazy smart and did everything he could to try and get us gigs and get us signed. He always had a fire up his ass and never gave up. Our band name started out as The Cage, then we all sat around one night smoking a thousand joints, putting ideas in a hat, and changed the name to Midnight Angel. I got that name from Pat Benatar's song Shadows of the night. I loved Benatar at that point and strived to be as great as her, but I had so many other influences in my voice. Olivia Newton-John, Donna Summer, Queen, and many other Disco singers from the 80s that I just loved, so I had a combo vocal. Midnight Angel stayed together for ten years.

We had a bunch of different members here and there, because of the usual drug issues back then, but for the most part, we had a solid core. I must mention our amazing bass player Brett who passed away back then from an overdose. He was one of the greatest musicians out there. What a beautiful human, yet unfortunately, he, too, had a lot of emotional issues.

Brett used to work at his dad's hair salon and would always bring me hair and nail products. I can't tell you how many times Gary and I would have to carry his past-out body up a flight of stairs, through the five n ten store that we rehearsed in, then across a very long parking lot, and into the car. Sometimes his body was so heavy we would have to leave him in the car overnight. He would show up out of nowhere as if all was good and go on with his day.

In 1996, Gary and a few friends started an E-Commerce business and asked if I wanted to join. I was so excited to finally be a part of something really cool, but I knew nothing about the internet. I had just previously learned how to use a Macintosh computer and how to work the desktop publishing gig for a magazine we both worked at before this. So, I was as raw as they come but anxious to learn. Gary tossed a book called Pagemill on my desk and said, "I need you to learn this."

I don't know how I did it, but it wasn't long before I was on the internet stealing code, writing code, and testing different ideas to launch live. One day at work, Gary called me and told me to come outside. We had to go to a funeral. I was not dressed for a funeral in white hot pants and a belly shirt, but he didn't care.

He told me when I got in the car that they found Brett dead from an overdose, and the funeral was today. I was so upset and utterly embarrassed to be around his entire family dressed like that. I'll mention that most of the guys in this band were Jewish, and I had this idea of their parents being uptight and judgmental, probably residue from the conversations at the dinner table with my family growing up. But to my surprise, Brett's parents were so happy that we were there and treated us like gold. They pretty much flaunted Gary and me around the house to their family as if they were proud to know us. And we spent hours in their basement talking about our great memories with Brett and some of our not-so-great memories as well.

I guess Brett couldn't hang on anymore. That was devastating. He wasn't the first friend I ever lost at such a young age to drugs, and unfortunately, he wouldn't be the last. By the time I was twenty-five, I had lost about 6 friends to suicide and drug overdoses. My first friend put a gun in his mouth and pulled the trigger. He was very depressed, but at the time, I couldn't help anyone out with my state of mind. That was tragic. I hate to admit it, but death doesn't really phase me much anymore. I can't even find tears much anymore.

R.I.P. Brett, you will never be forgotten.

One of the first real gigs we played was at the Stone Balloon in Delaware. We opened for Winger. At that time, I made a lot of my own outfits, and they all had a ton of bling on them. We all had crazy big hair, makeup, gaudy jewelry, and chains. Brett would come out on stage during Winger's sound check and tune his base. The guys who set up Winger's equipment were dicks and wanted Brett to get off the stage, but he wouldn't. Brett knew that they were just a hired group of lackeys, and because we had our own sound company, he knew that they didn't have any say, so he just stayed. He had balls!

He got so annoyed with their rockstar arrogance that he would sneak up and step on a peddle that controlled the smoke machine. The sound crew got really upset and tried to get us kicked out as Brett continued to step on the peddle and step on the peddle and step on the peddle. How would we know Kip Winger had asthma issues? Brett figured it was pretty stupid to have a smoke machine if your lead singer was asthmatic. He was like that, though, a complete pain in the ass, but he was our pain in the ass.

We played a bunch of cool clubs when rock clubs were around. One of my favorite gigs was at Atco Raceway in NJ, opening up for a WWE wrestling match with Joe Bonadonna hosting and The Samoans tag team and many other wrestlers that I can't name off the top of my head. We had a blast and signed autographs at the end of the night. But after ten years of making no money, spending hours, months, and years in the studio recording one album Midnight Angel Live at Fantasy Theater. The band was at the end of its time, and I wanted to get out there and make some cash, so I gave in to the cover scene. I "sold out," as any original musician back then would say. But I needed the cash because I had to pay rent.

For a little while, I auditioned for other cover bands and pretty much got every job other than one group that wanted a more polished wedding band singer. They called me months later when the perfect vocalist didn't work out, but I started working with a producer on a dance music album for about a year until he gave me a contract saying the record company pretty much owned me. The writing was much better than my first contract, but I didn't trust it and went my own way.

Later, I joined a band called the Exceptions and made bank, but unfortunately, my new boyfriend, soon to be my 1st marital debauchery, at the time felt the need to come to every gig, including weddings, and the band wasn't having that, so I had to leave after only being there for almost two years. It was ok though. I wound up divorcing him six months later, as mentioned later, and started my own band.

There was always an unspoken code in bands. See nothing, say nothing, and act like nothing ever happened. It was hard to be the only female watching some of the guys leave out the back door to get a blowjob from some random groupie, but there was that unspoken loyalty rule. Being friends with their wives was especially hard at times. It made me hate men even more because, again, I could see firsthand that they couldn't control themselves when there was a hot chick around. And there was an abundance of them.

Gary was always there to help me get started. He allowed me to audition musicians in the five n ten rehearsal room. I wanted Gary to be my guitar player, but he had no interest in playing cover tunes. From there, I had many pretty great cover bands. I did all the marketing, networking, set lists, and auditions, and I had my own booking agent, Freddie Baker, the best out there at the time. He had us booked out the wazoo! I ran the show and paid my guys every night for their great work. I must thank Gary for the training. He taught me so much from the business and music end of things.

Ten years of free, on-the-job training pretty much every day made me a great vocalist with a great business mind. Well worth it in every way.

I went on to start a band called Revolution Maker which was one of my favorite bands with some of the most talented and cool musicians. That was in the 90s when there were so many awesome female-fronted songs out there for me to sing. Then on to my duo Reds n West with one of my favorite male vocalists Steve West, now living out his singing career in Nashville. And then on to the last cover band I started, Fire Bush. I could go on about all my band experiences, but I think the picture is pretty clear.

Rich, Doug, Mike, Brett, Steve, and Me

I worked hard, played a ton of gigs, made a lot of money, and in my mind, was a rock star. That was my identity; people all over knew who I was. We got fan mail, signed autographs, and lived the rockstar life most of that time until it was over. No, we did not get as far as an MTV video back then, but we lived and breathed music. So, when I lost my voice in February of 2011, I was devastated and completely broken. But to give you a heads up, I got my voice back.

After leaving my stepmother Diana's house, I moved back to South Philly and rented an apartment that overlooked the famous Melrose diner and The Philadelphia Music Company. This was my 2nd apartment in South Philly over time. I had a decent job working in classified advertising for Focus Magazine with Gary and had a pretty good life on my own. But my friends were always trying to hook me up with someone, and I was kinda done for a while, but that didn't stop them. They picked me up one night and had a stray friend in the back seat next to me. I didn't think anything of it at the time, but it got a little weird. He introduced himself as Hutch, whatever.

He seemed nice enough, but I wasn't amazed or even moved by his personality. I thought nothing until my friends asked the next day. I'm wondering now if I was underdeveloped as a baby. Maybe from my mom smoking during her pregnancy, I don't know, but God, I must have been unconscious through the first twenty-five years of my life, seriously!

Let me start by saying that my first marriage lasted six months. I was twenty-five years old, and I wasn't ready or in love. Hutch and I dated for about three years, and we had some fun, but I wasn't over the moon about him. I never looked at him and thought, what a good-looking man or wow, I'm so lucky to have found him. I was just living life and going through the motions. I felt guilty about not wanting to get married because I found out that Hutch went to my father and asked for his permission to marry me. He had balls; I'll give him that much!

My dad told him he was a bum, a freeloader, and to get a friggen job.

I was so worried about making everyone else happy that I never put myself first or put my foot down when I knew something was a mistake or didn't feel right. I let people walk all over me, and I let the guilt trips take over. The mindset of a person who has been programmed and controlled for years by the programming of The Parents.

I'm still amazed at what I put up with. I went through the whole wedding circus charade and paid over fifteen thousand dollars for that and for my own honeymoon. Hutch didn't have a dime to contribute. I didn't really care too much about the flowers and the decorations, so I handed that over to the "mother-in-law-to-be" since she was absolutely ecstatic about preparing for her young King's wedding. I was so stressed out I didn't care.

I had to have my dress taken in at least four times because I lost about 20 pounds, and I was down to a size zero, two weeks before the wedding. I was one hundred pounds of skin and bones and all kinds of stressed out. My father hated Hutch so much that he told me he wouldn't walk me down the aisle or do the father-daughter dance with me at my wedding.

Thinking back now, I understand why my father was so adamant about me not marrying this jackoff. I just thought he was being mean as usual and wondered why he always hated me.

My dad wasn't a wordsmith, that's for sure, but he was right. A minute before we walked down the aisle, he leaned in and said that I could back out at any time, and he was serious. I couldn't imagine doing that because so many people were involved and so many people came to the wedding. That would be a horrible thing to do. What would people think? Guilt trip, guilt, guilt, guilt trip.

If you asked me now, it would be a completely different show. I would have walked down the aisle and whispered, "we're just gonna skip to the party part." But back then, I believed I had to force myself through this. It was my ego not wanting all the crappy people in my life to be right for once. Jesus, no one should be getting married at twenty-five! I thought I had my shit together and knew what I was doing. Nope, I was clueless! A thing not so easy to admit back then.

I can still clearly see myself all dressed up in this beautiful Victorian-fitted lace gown. My hair was professionally styled, my nails were sparkly perfect, and there I was, crying my eyes out during the entire ceremony. I must have blown my nose at least a hundred times, and I felt so sick to my stomach. I'm shocked that no one said a word when the priest asked if there is anyone here who thinks this is a big fucking mistake. Please speak now?!?

I guess everyone just figured I made my own bed, so I could lay in it. Because you know that not many people will tell you the truth until after the divorce is final, that's when they come out of the woodwork. Thankfully the reception was amazing, with great food, great music, and lots of booze. I did a lot of shots that night! I needed to be completely numb to deal with what I had just gotten myself into and what I was about to deal with moving forward. The rest of the night was a blur.

Needless to say, my first marriage was built on a guilt trip and had nothing to do with love. It only took a few weeks after we were married when my husband Hutch, ugh, just saying this makes me want to hurl. Hutch wanted me to be with women. When I first started seeing Hutch, I was singing full-time, and there were a lot of women who weren't into men at my gigs, and I sang a lot of popular female songs. I got along well with most of the women and men that followed my band at that time and moving forward. Often a few of the women would ask me out or to come back to their place after work.

I can remember this one beautiful girl who was around twenty-five, waiting for me in the lady's room of a club I was performing at. When I got off stage and went to the lady's room to wipe the lipstick and sweat from my face, she told me, with tears in her eyes, that she was in love with me and wanted to take me back to her place. I was like, "WAAAA" ??? I'm pretty sure she was high, and she knew I was married as I had a visible human attached to my hip, but apparently, she didn't care. I was so amazed at the fact that she liked me because, to be honest, most women outside of the club scene didn't like me.

I don't know if it was because of the way I dressed, being on stage, or how I carried myself. But I really didn't believe any of it. I thought it was all a trick or a game. I didn't trust anyone. There was this thing I had to deal with for years, my mind and how I thought others saw me. Being hated by my own family and being bullied in school because of the way I looked and dressed didn't help my situation. I didn't understand fully why I was hated so much, which made me hate myself even more. I was always so damn insecure, but I wasn't about to change for anyone. "Ok, I digress again, sorry."

My husband, hawk - eyes - Hutch noticed that I have this girl situation going on because he was up my ass 24/7, so he decided that it would be a really fun plan if he could hook me up with a woman. His lightbulb idea was that we could take her home, and she and I could get it on while he hid in the closet and watched! No harm in that, he explained.

"Did he really, truly ask me this? Is he out of his mind? I need to get the hell out of dodge and dump his nasty ass!"

I lost whatever respect I had for this puppet and for myself as well because I married this shmuck! This was everything I NEVER wanted for myself. Listen, I don't care what anyone's sexual preference is. I'm not gay, but I see a lot of beautiful women out there, and there were moments when I was curious about what it would be like to be with women, but I've never been pulled energetically to it. I love men. I love their strength. I love the idea and feeling of being safe with a man. And I love a sexy male body with a nice head on it.

So not only was this dirtbag on dating sites for lesbians trying to find himself a buddy for his new wife, but he was also watching porn on a daily basis on my computer. What the fuck was I doing in this situation? (You'll see that question frequently in this book)

Before this relationship started, I was working, making a lot of money, and I had my own place. But because he wouldn't work, he wound up living with me, and then we wound up living with his mother and family in an effort to save cash to buy a house. Hmm, looks like I was following in my mother's footsteps unconsciously again. I truly cared about his family, but in the end, of course, they were loyal to him.

After about five months in, I told him I wanted a divorce. I couldn't do this anymore. I was so unhappy and so stressed out. The band I was in at the time gave me an ultimatum; they said if Hutch came to anymore gigs, they would have to replace me. He even came to our wedding gigs. I realize now that he was insecure and very controlling. His mom treated him like he was a king, so that didn't help. She enabled the shit out of him. But he made every situation out to be a joke.

Like I was crazy, and I wasn't really seeing what I saw. My eyes were deceiving me.

He was a complete narcissist, and I started losing myself again. He would follow me around everywhere with his arms folded, telling me when to smile and what to do next. He would check my pockets when the night was over, making it a fun thing to do as he talked baby talk while looking for money and phone numbers. I was oblivious at the time, but eventually, I started hiding my money.

One day I was having a meltdown because of the guilt I was feeling inside. I ran away and went to a friend's house and stayed for a minute. Unpacked my stuff and tried to shower, but her place was filthy, and I couldn't deal with that chaos on top of everything else, so I packed my stuff up, thanked her, and left. The guilt I had was so bad that I was contemplating suicide once again. I drove around for hours in a borrowed car another friend lent me because Hutch talked me into leaving him our bright yellow "Mustang racecar" as he would take over the payments. It was easier to give it to him and run while he was being coddled by his family since the story he gave was that I was a lesbian.

That got a lot of attention. I still, to this day, find it hard to believe that they believed him. I thought they really knew me, but I understand that a lot of people are into the whole "blood is thicker than water" thing, so as my son would say, "it's whatever." By the way, he is another one who bragged about being Italian but with only a very small spec in his blood.

I figured I was a complete failure for sure now, and it would be best to go for good, so I bought a few boxes of sleeping pills since I knew that ninety aspirin didn't do the trick the first time. I sat for a minute and downed all the pills while parked in the parking lot in front of my friend Gary's apartment. I was out of my mind and not thinking clearly. I just sat in the car crying and obviously feeling like shit and felt sorry for myself, but I was ready to go. Then it hit me; I had to say goodbye to my best friend Gary, so before I was feeling the effects of the drugs, I gave him a call and told him I had to speak to him, and it was important.

He and I talked. I cried and told him about the deal with Hutch and that I had left after telling him I wanted a divorce. Gary knew about Hutch and didn't like him much at all but never tried to interfere. I started to pass in and out of consciousness. Gary was worried, and his girlfriend Lisa started asking me if I had taken something. I wouldn't answer other than, "I have to go now," but eventually, they pulled it out of me. My vision was fading. My body was fading rapidly, so they took me to the emergency ward. I was wheeled in immediately and asked many questions, which pissed me off because I didn't want to be there!

The big question came from a random nurse, "Suzanne, did you try to kill yourself?" I was a true dick in that moment and replied, "yeah, I tried to kill myself, so why don't you just let me get this over with?" And all of a sudden, that segment of my life completely changed.

Did you ever have a fat tube shoved up your nose, then down behind your throat into your stomach, then charcoal pumped in and pulled out? Well, if you believed I wanted to die before, that thought was even greater during this process. It was traumatic, to say the very least, and I was freaking out because it was painful, and they were holding me down. I was terrified and freaking the hell out. About an hour later, an officer showed up.

They put me on another gurney and strapped my hands and feet down, shoved me into an ambulance, took me to a different hospital, and locked me in a small room with a tiny bed and no sheets. It was so cold; I was in a hospital gown with no underwear, locked in what felt like jail. I completely lost my noodles and started banging on the door and screaming to let me the fuck out. I even took a chair and tried to break the wired glass window on the door until someone from security came in and told me to calm down.

"Calm down; you took me against my will and locked me in here." I was screaming bloody murder, so they warned me that if I didn't calm down, they would have to strap me down. I could hear Gary and Lisa's voices echoing from far away, trying to talk to them. I know they felt horrible after that, but I'm glad now they did what they did.

They wouldn't transfer me to a different facility until I was evaluated by a psychiatrist. Finally, after hours of sitting in this freezing cold room, the psych doc arrives. Questions: When you think of an apple, what comes to mind? Answer: Fruit. When you think of an orange, what comes to mind? When you think of clouds, what comes to mind? I was like, "dude, are you kidding me?" And off I go to the funny farm. I was there for about 2 weeks, and I was so angry with everyone. It was a crazy house in my mind, and I wasn't crazy. I just wanted to die.

I had zero rights, locked up with nothing but a hospital gown on suicide watch. Gary and Lisa went out of their way to call and check on me. They bought me clothes and underwear, a toothbrush, and whatever they could get me, so I started to feel like a human being again.

There was therapy all day and night, terrible food, and a lot of very sick people. I felt like such a loser especially standing in line at night for my meds. I was on anti-depressants for years and anxiety medication just to function. My whole life, all I thought about was how much I hated my parents and my shitty family and all of the shit I went through because of The Parents, and I could never break that feeling or forget those memories. It consumed my life every day.

I have very few "blood" family members I speak with now other than my children and my aunt TC, who happens to be my mother's little sister, and who my mother happens to despise. There was and still is a lot of anger and jealousy on my mother's part especially knowing that my aunt and I still talk and spent time together.

During my time there on the funny farm, Hutch and his mother came once to visit me. Just what I needed, my abuser and his mom coming to the crazy house to visit me. If his mom only knew that he was the biggest asshole! I really didn't want to see them because his mom was a pro-manipulator. I cared about her, but she was the head of the narcissist team. I couldn't wait till they left, but I had a feeling that she thought she could change my mind about her son. Eh, not happening. It took me a few days to calm down, but I did learn a lot there. Unfortunately, not enough to really stick, but it helped.

I was glad to get out of there, and Lisa was kind enough to offer me her basement to stay in for a while, so I didn't have to crawl back to my mother in laws house and deal with that nonsense.

After all that drama, we got through the divorce amicably, thank God. And in the end, after the divorce, his whole family thought that I left him because I was a lesbian. In fact, his mom met up with me to have me sign an agreement that I wouldn't take anything of his and vice versa. He had nothing to take. She also lectured me about her missing out on having a grandchild. Ugh, I was not the one for that. But when all was said and done, of course, they believed him, and of course, they all shunned me completely.

I had the attitude that I really couldn't trust anyone anymore, and I wasn't going to put myself out there or care about anyone romantically ever again. But that thought process didn't last very long. I was still unconsciously stuck in The Parent's program. And it just runs automatically over and over and over again. I've only told a hand full of people over the years what really happened in my marriage. Hutch tried contacting me on social media to tell me how great he was doing, and now he's a cop in Florida with a boat... That was the first day I learned how to block someone on Fakebook. WOW!

CHAPTER 13 | GORDON – "IT'S JUST A MATTER OF TIME"

Question of the day, how many times do I need to get beat down to realize that how I feel inside about myself is more important than the need for someone to love me? I just wanted to be loved. It was like I was on a mission my whole life to find someone, anyone, to love me and protect me, but in the back of my mind, there was no way in hell that this person existed. And who would I compare this spectacular person too? I had an abusive father who barely spoke to me. Every guy I dated was a cheater, a liar, a snake, a manipulator, and a fake, and was obsessed with porn, just like my father. Older guys were scum bags and liked little girls, and I couldn't trust anyone at all. This was what my mind was preaching to me sixty million times a day, yet I continued to attract the same bullshit over and over again.

My vibes were so pathetically low it was inevitable that only low-level-vibrating people would stick to me like glue. Like attracts like. But at the time, I had no idea about The Laws of Attraction, energy work, getting to know my inner self, or just learning to love myself first.

I never wanted to get married again, but eventually, I did it so my first son would have his father's last name.

Wow, now that's a really good reason to get married, right?

I was so naive and so misguided and utterly trapped in a beautiful young avatar body that housed this emotionally and dreadfully abused mind and spirit. Honestly, at that time, I truly believed my son and I would be fine whether I married or not, but his father convinced me that it had to be done. I'm not saying there's anything wrong with marriage, but for me, at least at that time, it wasn't anything I had ever really wanted because I didn't know one couple that survived marriage or had a good one at the very least.

I would say that my 2nd husband's abusive side was revealed after the marriage, but in all honesty, looking back years later, I saw the red flags, but I chose to ignore them and make excuses for him. I'll call him Gordon. I saw it when we were dating and chose to wear blinders because I didn't want to believe that I would ever be in a fucked-up relationship again. I didn't want to listen to my inner voice. I thought I was making shit up in my head.

"Was I really that dumb? Or was I just so fucking programmed by The Parents and their demonstration of a normal relationship that I couldn't break out of the chains that held me back for the first thirty years of my life? Well, I was about to find out yet again."

Our relationship was fun in the beginning. I cared about him and thought we could really make a beautiful baby together.

"Yep, that was my thought process. I don't know why, maybe the whole clock ticking thing, not really sure, but I wanted to have a baby, and I didn't want to get married. And the funny thing is that I specifically wanted a son. Damn, here I go again, following that pattern of conditioning that my mother had. I hated that she never spoke to me and that we had a terrible relationship if that. But what I hated more was the attention she gave to my brothers and how all she cared about was the men in her life, just like her mother. Crazy shit! And I still didn't change it."

My son's father, Gordon, agreed at that time that he did not need to tie the knot, but when our son was born and it came time for the official paperwork in the hospital, the nurse insisted that his last name be my maiden name since we were not married.

Fun quick fact, I just found out about 3 years ago that my maiden name was a complete lie, but I'll get to that later.

We both decided at that moment our son would carry his father's last name, which we managed to make happen, and then I was guilted into getting married about two months after his birth to seal the deal.

I know my kids wonder what our relationship was like because they were so young when we divorced, and it's really hard to explain, but I'll try without trying to hurt anyone. Gordon and I met at one of my gigs where he happened to work as a bouncer in a club the same weeknights that I worked for months, and eventually, he talked me into giving him my number. He used to come up to me after I finished singing and would say,

"Why don't you give me your number?" My response was, "that will never happen."

Gordon was about six feet tall, 250 pounds, with black hair, beautiful brown eyes, and a great smile, and Gordon knew it all too well. My gut and his weird mustache told me he was a scammer, but so far, listening to my gut wasn't a practice of mine. Then in a creepy whisper voice, he would say, *"It's just a matter of time, just a matter of time."* I can remember being up on stage and seeing him in the background smiling and saying that same line over and over again. "It's just a matter of time, just a matter of time."

I could read his lips and would just shake my head and laugh. It was annoying at first, but he got to me, and it became a cat-and-mouse game. Eventually, I gave in. As nauseating as this feels to me now, there was something exciting about this game. Little did I realize I was once again repeating the same old patterns that were programmed into my mind and my body by The Parents. Once again, I had to learn the hard way.

I really believe that while we are on earth as physical beings, we are here to play the "earth game." And whatever we overcome and learn puts us at a new level of expansion. But whatever we don't learn puts us into a hiccup state to repeat the same scenarios over and over, in different formats or experiences, maybe with different people, until we get it right. If we don't learn before we transition into non-physical, we will have to repeat these processes again when we come back until we get it right. It's all about growth.

At the time, Gordon and I were attracted to each other; and eventually, we fell in love and had fun together. We had a lot in common in the beginning, and we got along well. But both of us were damaged goods. At that time, I was in business with my friend Gary. We owned an e-commerce business, GoEmerchant.com, with a few other friends. I was still singing, and Gordon was working at HogenDaz stocking freezers with ice cream. We saved enough money to have our first house built in Delaware, but eventually needed to be closer to my business in New Jersey, so we decided in the year 2000 to have another house built while I was in the middle of carrying my twins Snuggs and Mammy.

My first son Bamm born in 1997, was around three years old when I became pregnant again, but after twelve weeks, I lost my baby. I was a mess, and it seemed like no one really understood what I was going through mentally or emotionally. I can remember the doctor asking me to try and scoop out the remains of my baby while passing. I couldn't imagine doing anything like that, and the thought of it horrified me. I drove home alone and cried for days. Life just goes on for sure. I held on to that loss by myself for a long time, never wanting to get pregnant again or risk going through that. But eventually, things changed, and by surprise, I was pregnant with my twins.

I was 200 pounds in my seventh month during that pregnancy. I struggled every day with extreme nausea, and walking and sleeping were real chores. Eventually, it got so bad that I had toxemia and begged to be induced. I can remember clearly calling my doctor and telling him my body was so swollen with fluid that I couldn't move or breathe. My legs were each about the size of my waist, and my face was unrecognizable.

I hadn't slept very much for months, and I was pretty concerned. It seemed like no one really heard me, but I couldn't go any further like this. Gordon was completely out of touch with any of it. I guess he thought I was complaining, but I knew something was wrong, and I felt like my body was going to shut down. There was no doubt in my mind that if I had gone any further with the pregnancy like this, someone would have had to decide between saving my twins or me.

Once I got to the hospital, Pitocin was administered, and I was given an epidural that did not take, and in a few hours, I gave birth to my babies. I watched as they took my new son Snuggs away first and then watched behind me with my legs in the air as they took my daughter Mammy to a different area of the room and started administering CPR. The doctor was cleaning me up, my son cried just a little, and my daughter was not breathing. I watched helplessly as Gordon put the video recorder down with tears in his eyes. I was scared shitless. No one would tell me anything other than, "Everything's fine. They'll be fine. "

After they took my babies out of the room, I was moved to another hospital room, where I passed out from exhaustion. I lost about 20 pounds of water that night, and my bed was soaked from sweat. I found out hours later that my babies were in the NICU with all kinds of issues. I didn't get to hold either one of them for weeks.

We were told that they weren't digesting properly, so they had to be fed through a tube in their belly. They couldn't breathe on their own, so they both had breathing tubes. My tiny son had to be on morphine because he kept pulling the tubes out. He had a small hole in his heart and jaundice. My beautiful little girl struggled to survive the whole time as well. It was a race, baby A versus baby B. One would do well, and the other would plummet, then vice versa. It was a roller coaster ride for a long time, and as much as I tried to stay calm, I was a complete mess inside.

There were many times when I thought I was going to lose them both, but the nurses continued to tell me to stay strong. They will pull through this. Oddly enough, we had the biggest babies in the NICU. Snuggs was 4.14 pounds, and Mammy was 4.9 pounds, both 22 inches long. Within about two weeks, I lost seventy pounds of pregnancy weight, and I couldn't see anything with a clear head. This was an incredibly traumatic experience for Gordon and me, living in the NICU while I pumped for milk every two hours, day and night, for weeks, praying that they would survive.

They had feeding tubes and IVs everywhere, so nursing was not an option. We couldn't even hold them. Baby A and Baby B are alone in incubators on each side of the room, with tubes and wires everywhere. It was one of the worst things I have ever experienced. I was over-the-top emotional. At least, that was what one of the nurses had mentioned to me. She said, "You may want to seek counseling." Well, duh, I had been living in the NICU with two tiny new babies watching them go downhill, then uphill every hour for seven weeks or so.

When you are in that environment watching your children and other tiny, tiny babies suffer all around you, some weighing only a pound, just lying there, or being transported to different hospitals because their hearts had stopped because their mothers were crack addicts and they didn't really have a chance, it gets to you. Don't get me wrong, the NICU nurses are incredible human beings, but that doesn't calculate in your brain while you're in the thick of it.

Thankfully both of our babies survived. In the meantime, my first son Bamm was there every day, just watching and asking questions. He was only four years old, and I couldn't imagine what his little mind was going through. I feel so bad that he had to go through all of that with us. I guess at the time, I thought it was better he got to be a part of it all and see his baby brother and sister instead of having babysitters watching him and keeping him from me.

My son Bamm with his big green eyes and beautiful smile was always very sensitive and kind. He was also pretty shy but very affectionate and caring, and he was my first child, my number one. Little did he know that his entire world was about to change. Bamm and I were very close, and he was truly the first human I had ever loved unconditionally. Children do that to you. They teach you a different kind of love and innocence. Nothing compares to that feeling. Bamm was with us every step of the way, and when it was finally time to hold and feed his little brother and sister, he was a true champ.

At this point, I never wanted to go through pregnancy again! Finally, after about seven weeks, we brought baby A home, so we were no longer allowed to stay in the NICU overnight. We were so happy and relieved to bring our baby home, but we still worried about our other baby making it. After about a week we got to take baby B home and start our new life with our newest additions to our family.

After all of that, months of being sick, weeks of worry, and the fear of losing my babies, I was good, and I really, really didn't feel the need to have more children. I don't think my body could have endured that again. Unfortunately, I found out later Gordon had different goals as he magically revealed that he wanted seven kids. Clearly, we never discussed this, and he became indignant about me getting my tubes tied. It was an issue for a bit as he vocalized that I was very selfish, but I still did it. It was done, and I was good.

By this time, we had so much on our plate. Two businesses, his sickly father, three kids, Gordon's first son, who was around seven at the time, a 70-pound Old English Sheep Dog named Cookie, a Persian cat named Beautiful, and a Cockatiel named Buttercup. And during all of this, we were working on the final touches to our new home day after day. It was very stressful for both of us, and we spent a lot of time taking care of everyone else day and night with no outside help. Neither one of us had any family that was interested in lending a hand.

I was working from home and not singing all that much anymore, and eventually, things started going downhill. My father-in-law was diabetic and had heart issues. He became ill as he got older and was not able to do much on his own other than go to the racetrack, McDonald's, or the store to buy lottery tickets and donuts. Gordon made it his mission to take care of him no matter what, but I didn't feel that tie as I was still very disconnected from any family other than my children. I don't think we were home very long after the birth of our twins when Gordon's father had to be hospitalized. And on top of everything else, his insurance didn't cover a nurse, so it became my job to set up his IVs every day.

Gordon and I worked like champs together the first year. The babies were not out of the woods yet, so we had to document every bowel movement, every meal, and every cry encountered to make sure they were thriving and healing. We had a strict routine where one of us would make the bottles while the other did the diaper changes. We did everything together, and we did it well. We knew that there was no other way to handle everything we had on our plates, so we just did what we had to do.

Looking back on it all now, more than twenty-five years later, it was way too much all at once, and Gordon and I started fighting a lot about everything. I would get really annoyed when he would lie on the couch and watch Nascar for hours while I was cleaning or taking care of four kids, three pets, his father, and doing laundry for seven people. And if he got sick, he was conveniently sick for at least a week, meaning he could do nothing but watch TV and eat.

I guess I always expected his help because I never felt like I had a break. Talk about jumping in headfirst! I don't really think I even had a concept of time back then. I was on autopilot 24-7. Learn as you go. After all, I kept telling myself I could take it. I could take anything because that's how I roll. "Go big or go home."

Clearly, I was good at the concept of finding and feeding a dysfunctional situation, but I had never seen a good relationship, let alone a woman, being treated like a human being at the very least. There were a lot of things I just didn't know. And slowly but surely, things got really bad to the point where Gordon started hitting me. It wouldn't be like a punch in the face or anything too obvious at first. It would be little jabs as he walked past me, or he'd block me in the hallway or wrestle me in front of the kids to the point where I couldn't breathe with his big body on top of mine.

Our kids would get scared and yell, "Daddy stop," but he would just laugh and say, "mommy and daddy are just playing." They knew instinctually that something wasn't right. I felt it too, but I couldn't believe it. I just thought he was big and stupid, and he didn't realize he was crushing me, yet at the same time, I could feel the switch in his personality.

This continued day after day, slowly more jabs in the hallway, more wrestling, more verbal attacks. Christ, I couldn't brush my teeth without him pushing my elbow in and saying, "what's the matter, can't brush your teeth?" Then he would look in the mirror and say, "I'm so damn good-looking." On top of that, he started beating our dog.

Our dog Cookie did not listen. He went through two weeks of dog camp training; I took him to one-on-one German dog training and even made a big poster of all the commands in German so the kids could learn how to train him. "Cookie Toma, Cookie Sitz" was all you heard in our house for months. Even the kids were frustrated after a while because he just didn't comply. But Gordon couldn't deal with the dog, so he would fist-punch him in the ribs or in the jaw.

Eventually, it got worse, and I had to choose between the family dog and Gordon, which was a struggle for me at that point. So for the safety of the dog, I managed to find a nice family in West Virginia who had a farm with goats and chickens. Cookie loved it there, and I felt better because he was safe. It was heartbreaking, especially for Bamm, but the fear of Gordon really hurting our dog was not ok. And I somehow thought that if I got rid of Cookie, Gordon's behavior would go back to normal.

I used to think incessantly about the consequences of divorcing this man. I thought about it for at least two years. How would this affect our children? What would I lose? How would I manage? Will I be able to support my children and the lifestyle we have on my funds alone? How would we work out visitation? Will my kids hate me, or will they understand that I was doing the best that I could in the situation I was in? Who would disown me afterward?

The normal mind chatter was consistent, and these were definitely things I felt I needed to consider. But at that time, I didn't have the guts to do anything. And to be honest, looking back on all of that now, none of it mattered because I found out firsthand that there is no way to control that outcome. You can have all the hope you want. You can pray every day. And you can tell yourself the kids will know the truth, but there is absolutely no way to control any of it. All you can do is take things one day at a time, one moment at a time, and hope for the best outcome, always staying true to yourself.

My mind kept telling me, "You're putting your kids through the same shit you went through; you need to get out of this marriage now before it's too late. You're just like your mother; you're going to ruin them just like The Parents did to you. You're just like your mother."

But I couldn't figure out which way to go. I felt like, maybe, the longer I waited, there was a chance that either things between us would work themselves out or I would walk away, and somehow it would be better. It was a major push-pull decision for me. On the one hand, I didn't want my kids to go through a divorce. I didn't want them to have to see their dad on a visitation day and miss time with him or have to choose which holidays they could spend with either of us. Yet, on the other hand, I didn't want them to witness the fighting and dysfunction or believe any of that was ok or normal. I really thought I could handle it.

After a while, I noticed Gordon's behavior changing drastically. I started finding things unexpectedly, like an email from a woman with three kids saying, "You sound like a great guy, and I'd love to meet you, but unlike you, I have three children that have football and cheerleading, so it's hard to schedule any me time."

I had such a knot in my stomach that I was sick. I was also pissed off but, in a way, relieved because this was my out. I replied to her, explaining who I was, what side of the bed I slept on, how much my share of the bills was, how many kids we had, and that she was welcome to move in as soon as I divorced this man. That same night, while I was making dinner and Gordon was in the office, I quieted myself down, waiting for some kind of response as I knew he was checking his emails.

I could sense that he knew what I did and heard him say, "you're an asshole," under his breath. My guess was that he had read her response. Finally, I had the guts to tell him I wanted a divorce.
We can stay friends for the kid's sake, he can see them anytime he wants, and we will split everything 50-50. HAAHAHAHAHAHHA WOMP!

I thought I had it all together, no problem. After that, all hell broke loose. I started looking at the bills more often and finding things like porn rentals and odd phone numbers. That made me even angrier. If there is one thing, I hate more than a lot, it's my man watching porn on the down low.

To me, it's an insult to any relationship, and it's sick. I don't want to be with anyone who sneaks around watching other human beings F each other in every area of the body that has an opening. The fact that you would have to sneak should speak volumes to anyone. I don't understand it, and I don't want to. In my opinion, your integrity goes out the window, and I want nothing to do with that. I think watching porn skews everything about what making love actually means and how it's practiced.

Wow, here I am, ranting again. This is funny. I guess another personality of mine is seeping out.

Yes, I'm sure there are people out there who have wild sex and do things outside of the box, but I don't think porn stars are a fair depiction of what it's really like. Not all women look like that. Not all men have 10-inch weaners. And I wonder how any guy would feel if their woman preferred watching porn to lying with them.

He's been playing me a fool for how long now? He started going out a lot, leaving me alone night after night. There was a chunk of time when he disappeared for twenty-nine days with his best friend, but I didn't know where he was. I called him over and over again to make sure he wasn't dead. Plus, I was alone with all of this responsibility, and it wasn't easy.

After about three days out, he finally answered and said, "I'm not dead," then hung up. He was hanging out with his friend in the casinos. One night when he did come home from his getaways, I went through his car and found a pair of panties in the glove department. I don't really even know what made me look in there because I was done, but I did. He laughed and said they were for me, but they were about two sizes too big. I'm guessing they were for the woman with the three kids. I was losing my mind. I was so fucking upset at how fucking stupid I was. I can't even explain how disgusted I was with myself and with him.

I'd dealt with a lot of abuse for years, but I was done! I was done a long time ago, but I stayed because I was brainwashed into believing that this is what people in these situations do because that's all I had ever seen. Looking back on all this right now as I write and hope to sleep soundly tonight, I was so emotionally damaged and so brainwashed with other people's beliefs and rules that I couldn't move in my own body. I should have packed my kids up and left a long time ago, but I had nowhere to go. And I had no one I could ask for help.

I was so fucking worried about what it would do to my kids because everyone I told this to just said, "you should try to work this out for the kids." I told my dad, and he said, "you're an asshole. I swear if you get divorced, you're an asshole." (His words exactly) "You will lose everything." I did, and I did. I went for a divorce, and I lost everything, but I'm jumping ahead of the story here.

One night after "the 29th night not coming home binge," Gordon walked into the house, went right upstairs, and stayed in the bedroom the entire weekend. I slept with my kids and only went into the bedroom to get clothes, but I knew something was really wrong, and obviously I was completely stressed out. He was on something; he wasn't right in the head, so I stayed away and focused on the kids. By the end of the weekend, I decided, "Fuck this; I'm sleeping in my bed." It was one of the longest nights of my life, yet it all happened so fast.

Gordon was watching TV in the bedroom, so I turned my lamp on to read. We argued back and forth, "turn the light out, no, you turn the TV off, no, you turn the light out," and then he lost it. I was exhausted, and that didn't turn out the way I had planned, and within minutes I saw my entire life flash in front of me and learned how to grow a tiny set of balls.

Before I could really grip what was happening, all 250 pounds of Gordon's body was on top of all 110 pounds of me, foam in the corners of his mouth from using, and while he held a pillow over my face, he was yelling, "I'm going to fucking kill you bitch."

This was the first time I was afraid, really afraid. I kept asking myself why the hell I stayed so long. I realized then that I had no idea who or what I was married to. I had no idea what was about to happen to my kids and me. All I knew for sure was that I didn't want my kids to ever have to go through anything remotely close to what I went through when I was younger, but that completely backfired on me. I had spent eleven years with this man, but I had no idea what was about to happen.

I couldn't breathe, and I couldn't get his big 250-pound body off me. He was crushing me as he held the pillow over my face, and I was trying to fight back, but I couldn't move. He made a quick shift to try and hold my arms down with his knees, and something took over my body. I was fully conscious that he was going to kill me. And out of nowhere, I managed to knee him in the nuts, and as he let go to grab them, I kicked him off the bed and dialed 911.

If you are addicted to drama, insecure, and afraid like I was, you'll know what I did next. I hung up the phone. Yes, I did! I hung up the F'ng phone! WTF????

In the meantime, our kids were in their rooms. Three little children had to hear all of that. It's fucking sad, to say the very least. Once again, my programming held me down in this restricted, low-energy bubble. All I ever knew when watching my mom get abused was that she did nothing but beg for her abuser to stop. She didn't seem to care that my brothers and I were there in the same room watching it all moment by moment. Maybe she couldn't see us because she was traumatized. I don't know. If anything, she would be angry at us for being there after all was said and done. No kid should ever have to see that.

The police traced the call and came right over. It was so physically draining that I couldn't think clearly. I suppose I was in shock, and afraid, and I couldn't answer their questions. I was so used to abuse from my childhood and most of the people I grew up with, that my first response to the officers was, "I'm good, I'm sorry to bother you guys, I'll be fine. I'm sorry to bother you. I'm sorry to bother you. I'm really sorry to bother you."

"Man, I am writing this and remembering it all like it was yesterday, but I meditated before I started writing, so I don't have to fear going to sleep tonight. Seriously!"

I was around thirty-nine years old or so, and although I hate that I was so weak and beaten down emotionally, I've learned over time to have more compassion and love that brave little girl inside of me who fought most of her life to stay around.

"Christ on the Cross," how could I not know better? I wished I was dead most of my life but didn't have the balls to really pull it off.

A lot of people think that when someone tries to commit suicide, they are looking for attention, but, in all honesty, I assumed each time that I would succeed. I sometimes feel like my attempts failed because I had a higher purpose and that there was more for me to do here on earth.

If one of my friends had come to me with this story and needed help, I would have done everything in my power to get her or him out, but I had no one. My family had no money, and they weren't there for me. I was living this humungous lie. I had two businesses, the house, the kids, the husband, the money, and the Mercedes. I even pretended to enjoy and be interested in going out to the neighbor's house once a week with the other mothers in my development to watch desperate housewives in my flannel jammies, play board games, drink wine, and eat cookies. Even though I hated it, I just wanted to fit in so badly.

My reality was that I couldn't manage to attract a good human being if I tried. And I don't think I ever really knew what it was like to enjoy and love my life as I do now.

The police took some info and left but told me to call them if anything else happened that night. I went back into the house, embarrassed and exhausted, and my body was sore. I grabbed one of the kid's single mattresses and drugged it down into my office and locked the doors. I figured it best not to be in the same room as the kids just in case because I kind of knew it wasn't over. I called my mom to tell her what was going on. She listened to me cry hysterically, but she didn't help me. No one could help me, or at least that was what I believed. About five minutes into my call, Gordon busted into the office in the dark, making Hulk-like noises.

He grabbed my phone and threw it across the room, grabbed the mattress, and flipped me off it. I was screaming for my mom to call the police, but she didn't. I don't know what she did, but I got up, ran upstairs, and called the police again. He was too slow to catch me. This time I told them what he did. He tried to kill me.

It didn't take long for them to arrive, and he heard what I told them and started pacing, saying I was nuts and they would never believe me. He was such a manipulator, but I knew he was afraid. The police came, I told them everything, and then they spoke to him. They were concerned because he was acting strange and slurring his words. His story was that he had taken a few of my Xanax prescribed to me for anxiety. He said he never touched me and to ask his thirteen-year-old son, my stepson J who was there with him the whole time but wasn't. That was a complete lie, of course, but later I was told that his son confirmed what his dad told him to say.

My stepson J was about four years older than Bamm. J was always a kind, loving, affectionate little boy. I was very close to him for the first ten years, and he was the first child I ever had from someone else's relationship. He loved his father dearly and would do anything to get his attention, but unfortunately, Gordon preferred that his father take care of him for the most part. I felt so bad for this child when he was little because Gordon would yell at him all of the time or beat him for no real reason. There was a time in the past when I witnessed Gordon giving him a beating with a belt because he was afraid to sleep in the bedroom where Gordon's mother had passed years prior.

I also watched as he grabbed this child by his tiny arms and squeezed so tight that he left bruises in the shape of his fingers. I stood in a corner, almost paralyzed as I watched but quickly snapped out of it to tell Gordon if I ever saw him lay his hands on J again, I would call the police. The worst part is that this all happened before I got married, so I clearly saw the signs but still moved forward.

A paramedic checked me and saw all the bruises I had. I told them I was ok but wanted him out. I feared for my children and our lives. I told them I wanted to press charges. And as all this was taking place, most of our neighbors were out watching the show. Just like when I was a kid. The thought of repeating the same damn patterns my mom did, never even came to mind, but there I was. Over and over again, like a good, brainwashed zombie human cowering in a corner, just waiting for it all to be over.

The police took Gordon to the station to get a statement. They asked me to come in a different car to get a statement as well and told me that they could only keep him away for 24 hours. That I don't get! Once I got to the station, a female officer asked me to undress and took pictures of my face, arms, legs, and back. I didn't even know I had black and blue marks all over my body. They asked me if I was sure that I wanted to press charges, and I said yes. All I could think about was my kids watching this, crying for their Daddy to stop.

I returned home exhausted and not able to sleep. On the one hand, I wanted him to burn, but on the other hand, I still wasn't sure if I was doing the right thing. Even after everything that had happened, I still found a way to feel bad for Gordon. I thought that meant that I had a good heart, but I realize now that I was so abused at this point that I didn't know how to think outside of the box or put myself first.

Days later, he came back to the house, and I was just sick with worry and fear. We avoided each other as much as possible for a while. There was a lot of silence. A few weeks in, when I was leaving to go to the store, he followed me into the garage and tried to talk some sense in me. He got down on his knees in front of the garage doors and begged me not to end the marriage. He tried to assure me that he would change. I told him the only way to try and save anything was for us both to go to therapy, but he refused, yelling that I was the crazy one.

I was done, and he was pissed off.

We finally had a court date, and the prosecutor walked me through the process, including what would happen, that he would most likely go to jail, etc. Of course, I was alone, as usual, to handle all of this while my kids were being watched at home. Minutes before the hearing, he asked if he could speak with me. "No way bud, no way." The prosecutor pulled me aside and said, "If you talk to him, he will try to get you to drop the charges. I see this all the time, and the outcome will be worse for you down the road. He will not change."

And here comes the heavy wave of guilt and curiosity about what Gordon wanted to say to me. Curiosity killed the cat, they say, and I was the cat.

"I want to make a point really quick. This is what a lot of abuse victims do when all we know is our programming. We unknowingly do what our parents or the people we surrounded ourselves with would have done or had done already. Walking zombies, I mean, there was always a little voice inside me telling me to do the opposite, but that guilt trip was hardcore, and I didn't listen. We tend to feel bad for our abuser and go against our gut because we wouldn't want to hurt anyone or make them feel the way we feel."

I thought there had to be another way, but I didn't know how to do it. Even though all these people, the prosecutor, and the police wanted to help me, I didn't know them from squat, and at this point, I didn't trust anyone. They didn't know my situation, and who were they anyway? Very quickly, it all went downhill.

We went into a private room, and once again, Gordon got down on his knees and begged me to drop the charges. "Please, I'm so sorry. If you go through with this, the kids will grow up without a father. Don't do this, don't do this to them, please." He was in tears, and I actually felt bad. Within seconds, and out of nowhere, I forgot every single thing that he had done to me. It was as if none of it was real. I went back and told the prosecutor that I couldn't go through with this. My kids won't have their father. I can't do that to them.

I felt the blood drain from my head to my toes while she begged me to listen to her and not let him manipulate me. But I did it, and I dropped the charges. WOW! And that was the very beginning of the next thirteen years of a different kind of torture.

He came back home, and we slowly started to act as if nothing had ever happened. We went to a mediator to discuss splitting everything up without a lawyer, time with the kids to be more than 50-50, he could see them anytime he wanted, I didn't need child support, and we agreed to split whatever the kids needed and on and on. I thought it went well, and we agreed on all areas. I actually believed that we could do this and that we were on a better path and could possibly be friends, at least for the kids. We put the house up for sale mainly because Gordon said if he couldn't live there, then we couldn't live there. We started packing and started selling all of our furniture. There was an auction and tons of random people roaming through our home carrying out our furniture for pennies. Thousands and thousands of dollars and furniture were pretty much given away.

The house slowly started emptying. And every dime I made from this, I split with him, no questions asked, all cash. But it was still torture. I went around the corner to my friend Lee's house, and I told her what was going on. I mentioned to her in the middle of our conversation that I was contemplating crashing into a tree before I arrived at her house. I was just being me, saying exactly what was on my mind as I was trained to do, but she was concerned, so she took me to the hospital just to get checked out as I was so weak and skinny, down to 100 pounds and looked horribly sick. While we were there, she told someone that I was suicidal, and she was worried, and once again, I was hospitalized for a week against my will on suicide watch.

Lee stepped up and watched our kids that week until I came home while their father went to work. I saw Gordon entering the hospital while I was being evaluated, trying to come in to see me, but I refused to visit him. I also refused any calls coming in. I didn't want to speak to anyone at all, especially my mother.

I was angry with Lee for doing that, but I can appreciate it now. I was mad that I had no family to help me, even though I thought I had a family. That was all bullshit. I was sick of myself for being so weak, and I just needed to be alone but being alone was not an option there. This place was filled with all types of people, from mental illnesses to drug addiction, just like the other places. Here we go again. I went in with only the clothes on my back, and they had a strict schedule for me. Shower at six am if you want a shower, breakfast at seven am or you don't eat, group exercise for twenty minutes, and about seven different therapy sessions up until ten pm. Then you stand in line for your meds. You know the drill. At this point, you can probably tell that medication and therapy didn't help me.

I couldn't sleep to save my life due to my past work schedule and having three children who would only sleep if they were in bed with me for so many years. The only thing that kept me from wanting to die was the thought of my children having to live with that story for the rest of their lives. Eventually, I was back home, back to normal, unloading my life and everything I owned to the public.

During the divorce process, Gordon managed to steal all of our clients from our credit card processing business and emptied our bank accounts. He was a master manipulator, abusive, narcissist-bully-con-man, and cheater. Oh wait, he's just like my dad. Go figure.

But despite everything that he put me through, I still somehow managed to be loyal to him. At one point, my father-in-law accused Gordon of stealing his credit card after he returned from a week-long visit in Florida with his other son, Gordon's brother, who, by the way, always hated me for some reason and was very jealous of Gordon. At the time, I couldn't believe what I was hearing. After all, we spent years taking care of Gordon's father. I was so insulted after everything we did for him that he would have the kahunas to accuse his own son of such a thing. And to be honest, there was a part of me that thought that all of this nonsense was simply coming from Gordon's brother and his jealousy.

Out of anger and exhaustion, and just being fucking tired of this whole shit show, I told Gordon's father to pack his things and leave our house. I thought it very strange that Gordon never stopped me. After all, it was his father. But he sat there in silence and went along with it. I'm pretty sure my stepson J wanted nothing to do with me at that point because that was his pop-pop. The man who practically raised him when he wasn't with his mother. About a week later, I confronted Gordon, and he admitted to me that he did steal the credit card. He didn't know why, but yes, he did steal it.

Not too long after that, our house was sold, and I wound up buying a house in a different area of NJ, not knowing it was seven minutes from my now ex-husband's new girlfriend's house. I figured she was the one with the three kids Gordon was contacting while we were married, but I'm not convinced. My guess is that he was talking to a few different women. At this point, his girlfriend, I'll call her Roman, who I would describe as being a heavy-set, shorter woman who is very hard, obnoxious, dysfunctional, controlling, and a calculating narcissist with brown hair and freckles, started parking at the top of my street in her blue truck for hours stalking me. My new neighbors were knocking on my door, asking if they should call the police or not. She freaked me out, she was psycho, and that's being gentle.

I guess she was protecting her new prize a few weeks after his divorce. But believe it or not, over time, Gordon and I were able to be civil for the kid's sake, almost as if nothing ever happened.

I have this handy shut-off valve inside me that comes and goes. And once I'm completely done with someone or something, I could shut them or it off in minutes and never go back. Unfortunately, history shows that I didn't exercise my shut-off valve wisely for a long time.

Roman, his girlfriend, wasn't having any of that. Gordon would come over to my house to see the kids daily and let me listen to psycho voice messages from Roman about not wanting to be his weekend sex object, to put it nicely. He thought it was funny, and I thought, shit, you are in a bad situation, bro. After she kicked him out and broke up with him pretty early on, he asked me if I could help him out for a bit. I actually let him stay in my house until he could get back on his feet. I WAS SO F'ING STUPID!!!

Honestly, at the time, I thought, why not? I could use some child support, and being civil and friends would be a good thing for the kids. No, it was not the best solution, but we were in the thick of it, trying to survive and move forward, and we both needed a helping hand.

I'm pretty sure you're wondering where the fuck my head was and that at this point, you may also be thinking I totally deserve everything I got, and you would be correct as far as I'm concerned, especially after unraveling my life and reliving all of my mistakes. But I wouldn't wish this on anyone's child or any human being. I may have been really insecure and naïve, but that doesn't give anyone the right to torture another human being or their children.

During this time, the fact that I had to endure about eight months of being stalked and hearing comments about the way I looked or what I was doing in my personal life by Roman, some random woman I knew nothing about, was nauseating and quite frankly her sick behavior was concerning to me. Roman even had the balls to tell Gordon that she didn't think our son Bamm was really his. I knew I would have to deal with this devil for many years to come, but I sure didn't want to deal with her living five miles from my house.

I put the "For Sale" sign up on that house and got the hell out of there as fast as I could. Yes, another move! I decided to have a townhome built back in our old neighborhood in Swedesboro, New Jersey because I thought it would be the best thing for my children. I figured that they would feel more comfortable, and they could be with their old friends, and it would make things better for them. And I simply could not stomach the girlfriend stalking me and watching my every move.

Yes, it was worth packing up again and getting out of dodge because I knew in my gut that there was something really wrong with this woman. The settlement on my new townhome was delayed last minute, but my house was sold, and I had already signed my kids up with their old school. This was not the best of situations, and I really had no idea what to do. I figured that we would have to stay with a friend for the week until the paperwork on the house was finalized. I told Gordon what I was doing and that it was time he went somewhere else. He was upset but seemed to understand, then followed up with a request for me to lend him five hundred dollars to help him find a place to stay.

I told Gordon I did not have an extra five hundred dollars to give and that he would have to find a way to do this on his own. He was persistent in his request, but I didn't have it, and he was not happy about that.

That week was the worse week of my entire life.

March 5th, 2007, a date that was celebrated yearly with cake by Gordon and Roman with our children as a special family day.

I got a call from the kid's dad saying he wanted to see them for the weekend, which I thought was fine and would definitely make things a little easier, being that my life was in storage at the time and that I would be moving into my new townhome in a week. I kissed my kids and said, "Mommy will see you guys in a few days." About ten minutes after he picked my kids up and left, he called me, and in his creepy whisper voice, he said, *"You'll never see your kids again."* Here we go. I knew that whisper shit would come back to haunt me one day. I lost it and started freaking out, but he kept saying the same thing repeatedly. *"You'll never see your kids again; you'll never see your kids again."*

I swear to God, his voice was chilling as if he was auditioning for some kind of sick, psycho movie. I can remember clearly how loud I yelled Fuck You; I'll have you arrested, Fuck You!!! As if I had any power over the situation.

I screamed until I lost my voice. Guess I got that from The Parents. I'm confirming here that yelling and screaming all the time never solved anything. It just makes it hard to focus and be clear on your intentions. I understand now that my emotions are completely attached to my memories of trauma and that, scientifically, they cause a chemical reaction in the body and mind, unloading stress hormones that literally leave the thinking mind in an unstable and unthinkable state. Fight or flight. I only wished that I had understood this years ago as I believe that I would have had a better grip on my emotions, and I would have been able to think more clearly. But I didn't, and so I didn't.

My entire body was shaking from fear. I became paralyzed, and my mind could not process anything, much like most of my childhood. He was kidnapping my children, and I'll be damned if Roman wasn't behind the whole ordeal! I'll quickly note that you never want to deal with an irrational woman who's clearly unstable and willing to do whatever it takes, including destroying an entire family, in order to keep her man or simply feel in control. And in my opinion, Roman is a true narcissistic female with major emotional issues quite possibly worse than mine. Makes me wonder what her parents were like, although I think it's pretty clear.

I called the police, and they just rattled off that he has a right to visitation, so there was nothing they could do. I don't know about any other states or their rules about divorce and custody, but from what I do know, New Jersey rules are very different than Pennsylvania rules. Since Gordon and I agreed to have joint custody without specific time frames, the police repeated over and over that this is a family court issue, and he has every right to have the kids as well as me. Yet, if I went over there to see my kids, the police would force me to leave despite the unspecified visitation dates. So, the rules only apply when convenient.

And that's why ladies and gentlemen, you need to go broke and get a lawyer no matter what the cost! Being nice and being civil gets you ZERO in this type of situation. Although I still firmly stand against fighting in front of the kids, if it's at all avoidable. I know I sound like a broken record, but it's so hard for me to grasp how fucking stupid I was.

 I really thought that our agreement to stay civil meant something, but it didn't as long as he needed a place to stay and did what his girlfriend told him to do. This man has absolutely zero integrity. I immediately sensed that he had finagled his way back to her because, as much of a jerk as he was, this was not anything he would ever do on his own, at least from what I knew of him. Though I know there are always more than two sides to every story, and I hate what Gordon did to us, I still feel like he was following Roman's lead.

They were a tag team. Both of them are incredibly angry people, and they feed off of winning no matter what the situation or who it hurts in the end. Adults, children, friends, family members, it doesn't matter because winning, having things, and being right is what they live for.

To be completely honest, I've never met anyone as evil as them, and together they are everyone's worst nightmare. Together they have repeatedly destroyed so many people's lives with their manipulations, lies, and deceit. Nothing is too low for this couple. At one time, Roman even manipulated a situation where she had Gordon's Ex-wife, Stace's little girl, taken from her.

Roman was going to Stace's home to pick up Gordon's son J but couldn't keep her mouth shut and was harassing Stace.

Stace is about 5' 2" tall, a tiny little thing with blonde hair, funny, and very kind. Stace has zero tolerance for nasty people and wore imaginary body armor for 24-7 protection, as a lot of us do, from all of the issues she had dealt with over time.

When Gordon and I first got together, he brought me to Stace's home to pick up his son J for the weekend. Stace came outside that night to check out my car, and me of course. She had some words with me jokingly like, good luck to you, I already had him, hahahahaha, and so on. She is very straightforward and crass but also very loving and genuine. Not too long after that, Stace and I became friends. We even spent a few Christmases together with all of the kids at her house, where Gordon, Stace, I, and the kids would decorate, have dinner, sleepover, and record Christmas day with the kids.

She and I would frequently meet at her place for lunch, and she owned her own salon, so she would cut my boy's hair, never asking or taking a dime. I actually felt very connected to Stace and enjoyed her company. A lot of people would ask me if I really thought it a good idea to hang out with her, but I liked her, and I've always felt it would be the best thing for the kids if we all genuinely got along.

Stace warned Roman about being on her property and starting trouble with her in front of her son J a few times. Roman and Gordon probably have no idea of the damage and hurt they put on this woman, this mother. They calculated a plan to take Stace's little girl away from her. And they warned Stace that they would do it if she didn't comply with whatever deal they were offering to her about J. To be clear, they didn't kidnap her little girl, but their plan was to have the child's father believe the lies they made up in order to get him angry enough to take the child away from Stace through the courts. And they succeeded.

It's absolutely heartbreaking and unfathomable. Stace had called me out of the blue at around 3 am, hysterically asking me how I did it. How did you deal with them taking your children away? Unfortunately, Gordon and Roman had convinced Stace years before this incident that I was unfit as a mother and didn't want my kids anymore. Actually, I believe the story was that I left all three of my children on Roman's step one day because I didn't want them anymore.

That story was passed around for many years. I couldn't go anywhere to see my kids without everyone who knew Gordon and Roman or myself thinking that I dumped my three kids on Roman's step. This is a woman I didn't even know. A woman my ex had been dating for a few weeks. And this was a week after I had just had a four-bedroom townhome built in our old neighborhood. It's amazing to me the lack of loyalty that a lot of people have. It's amazing to me that the truth could be right in front of you, but it's easier not to think or break things down when they just don't make any sense.

Gordon could tell someone the sky is purple, and they would figure out a way to skew their internal color scheme to fit his narrative. Most of my friends and family questioned me on this as well, after being coaxed by Gordon.

I've always said he's the best salesman there is, no doubt about that. In fact, there was a time not too long ago when my kids asked me why I had abandoned them, as if they believed it. I had such a knot in my stomach because the idea that my children didn't remember what actually happened and that they were convinced of this story was torture. But I often remind myself that they were just ten and seven years old and that they were going through their own personal traumas for years.

I feel horrible for Stace because I know her kids meant everything to her, and she did the best she could as a single parent. She would go above and beyond for her kids, and now, after all the years of drama and torture, she has neither of them, and she's heartbroken. It bothered me a little when Stace alluded to the fact that she was unsure if I really left my kids back in 2007 because I thought she knew me better, but I understand from firsthand experience how manipulative Gordon and Roman are. Unfortunately, Stace had to get the truth the hard way, and though I have not been able to find her in about two years, I miss her, and my heart goes out to her every day.

I have no anger for Gordon and Roman anymore, as I understand now that this is their journey and that my journey is completely different. And believe me, it took years of isolation, meditation, and self-mastery work on my part. I still have a way to go as this "life test in earth school" seems to be ongoing, but I have forgiven them both, and I've moved on. I believe in Karma and know that sometimes the simplest of Karma could be the two of them being stuck with each other and alone at the same time for the rest of their days because it would be as if they were living with themselves. At the same time, I don't wish ill on either of them today. Karma will come to get them either in this lifetime or the next. It's out of my hands and I'm ok with that now.

After many phone calls to the police and being devastated by the calls to follow, I went to get my kids, but when I arrived at

Roman's home, no one would answer the door. I could hear my children crying and yelling for me, "Mommy, mommy," but one of Roman's sons kept them from the door. I could hear him talking on the phone to Gordon the entire time. In a few minutes, the police came and told me to leave. They said my ex has a restraining order on me, and I cannot be on their property. Again, the Blackwood, NJ police did nothing and continued to do nothing for over ten years. A few weeks to follow, we had a court date. Now I have to prove that I did not threaten or try to harm my ex. In the meantime, I still could not see my kids.

I got a job with a law firm a few weeks later and worked for a female lawyer in trade for her representation. But we had to wait weeks and weeks for a custody date. Gordon had been harassing me that month with phone calls, and again all in his creepy whispering voice. *"You'll never see your kids; you'll never see your kids again. What's it like to know you'll never see your kids?"*

He had harassed me with these calls over 350 times in less than a month. I found the time to print out my phone bill to bring it to court, as I wanted to be prepared. But when all was said and done, this was simply Gordon and Roman's way to buy time in order to get my kid's paperwork together and register them in a school in their area before I could get to court, and they succeeded.

Once we got to court, my ex told the judge that he feared for his life with me. She asked him how much he weighed and how tall he was, and suggested 280 pounds, roughly six feet tall; then asked me my weight and height, 110 pounds, 5' 4" tall. I gave her the phone records and told her the opposite was true and that he was harassing me. It was all too obvious to everyone that this was a joke, and the judge told him to get out of her courthouse and don't ever waste her time again. Yeah, my thoughts exactly!

Unfortunately, this hearing had nothing to do with them taking my kids, and I had to wait months for another hearing to fight for them. In the meantime, Gordon called and invited me over to Roman's house to say happy seventh birthday to my twins. This came with a price. They gave me a bunch of rules before I got there to make sure I didn't get any crazy ideas about trying to start trouble or discuss what was happening with them. I had no choice and went. I just needed to see my kids.

When I got there, they allowed me to come into the foyer and sit on the step. Gordon, Roman, and her three kids surrounded us as if to protect my kids from me possibly harming them. They were playing this act out 100%. It made me feel horrible, like I had no rights as a mother, and the look of disappointment on my kids' faces was terrible. I felt like a prisoner, as they watched my every move.

At this point, moving forward, Roman didn't want Gordon speaking with me unless she was there and felt it her duty to take charge and joined in bullying me for the next ten years in front of our kids, in public, behind closed doors, via text messages, at events if they allowed me to come, and face to face anytime she could. They did everything in their power to keep my children and me apart; cops, court, money demands, threats, screaming matches, "the works!" They would set me up to spend the day with my kids, but when I got to their home, no one would be there. They even left a paper towel with a rock on it at the step that read,

"Sorry, we didn't think you were coming, so we went to the beach. See you next time."

They have no soul at all, and as a mother, I can't imagine another mother doing that to someone. I made it my mission to get police reports every time there was an issue, but out of all the many officers I dealt with in New Jersey, only one did anything to help. It was like my ex had them all in the back of his pocket. So many years with my kids were stolen from all of us, and our relationship eventually became very strained.

The little things that most mothers could truly appreciate and look forward to, like your children losing a tooth, haircuts, talent shows, bedtime stories, dressing them, tubby time, hugs, naps, parent-teacher meetings, all the things that really matter to a parent, were stolen because of jealousy and revenge.

And this brings me to another rant.

What in God's name would possess a person to want to harm the relationship between a mother and her child or a father and his child? Can some people really be that angry and damaged that they feel the right or justification in some way to take a child from a parent? And for what? Was all of this done so that they could feel like they won? But after all of the manipulation and scamming and plans to destroy me, not at any time did these two people give a second thought as to what kind of damage they would be doing to not just my three kids but also the effects it had on Roman's three kids and my stepson J. Think about it, Roman moved my three kids and some guy into her home with her children and incorporated them into her life and her kid's lives. After only knowing this man for a few weeks.

Each one of her kids had to give up part of their bedroom, part of their dinner table, their shower time, and their mother to four strangers and deal with it because they had no say in the matter. It's interesting on the down low how Gordon got his wish back then to have seven kids. Be careful of what you wish for, I suppose.

The emotional, mental, and physical damage they inflicted on all of these little people, no doubt, are now trauma residuals left for all of them to have to work on in their adult lives and their future relationships. And that's the last thing I ever wanted for my children.

I was forty-one years young, fighting every day for a measly phone call with my kids, and if I was lucky to speak to any of them, it would only be if they had me on speaker so The Parents could chime in and listen. In the beginning, I would drive forty-four miles up and back a few times every week to try to see my kids, and there were many times that I was the only one who showed up. I would call and get no response because they took the kid's phones away.

It became standard procedure to sit in the parking lot for thirty minutes or an hour before they arrived, only to endure the next segment of torture before we could leave.

Gordon would get out of his car first and yell across the parking lot, most times with foam in the corner of his lips. "Where are you taking them today? You know the rules, right? What are your plans for helping out with college? Bamm is getting his license soon. Are you gonna buy him a car? You look like shit. You have bags under your eyes. Who are you dating now? Are you gonna start giving me extra money?"

When I tell you fucking torture, FUCKING, SICKENING, TORTURE!

I don't blame my kids for not wanting to go through this shit every week just to spend time with me. There were a few times when he didn't like my response, so he lunged at me. Fear would overcome my entire body, but I would have my cell ready and 911 on speed dial. In some cases, I wished that he would have just finished the job, but, in all reality, he was a big bully who hit women and children.

The amount of fear and stress I took on every time I drove there was too much for anyone to have to deal with. And every time my kids got in the car, they would be so stressed out that they would cry and fight with each other the entire hour's ride back to my place. Their father would yell and fight with me before they got into my car, and he would yell at the kids on the ride over about what they could and could not say or do when they were with me. And when I dropped them off, he would ask them a million questions and yell at them again. I used to pray to God that I wouldn't get in an accident while driving over the bridge because I would be shaking while all three kids were in the back seat fighting and crying.

It got to the point where they didn't even want to go through it anymore, so when my sons were old enough to work, it was the best excuse to get out of dealing with that shit, and I believe they used that as the reason they couldn't see me.

One Mother's Day, Roman was dropping my kids off at one of our many meeting places. She pulled her car up close, trapping me between my car and hers in a Walgreens parking lot. She decided it was time to let me know that she was their mother now. And told me that they gave her a Mother's Day card. I still can't believe I defended myself by reminding her that I made, carried, and gave birth to them. That went right over her head. If I bought them anything, she would take it from them or tell us all it was not allowed or inappropriate. I believe that "inappropriate" was one of her favorite words. It didn't matter what it was; if they had any pictures of me or us together, she would steal them from their room and keep them in a box in her bedroom. She had pictures of me and of my kids hidden in her box as well.

Fucken weird, to say the very least. I know this not only because my gut told me, and it was too obvious, but also because my daughter Mammy found them while snooping and sent me pictures to show me that I was right about her. If I picked my kids up from their house, Roman would stand at the front door petting and kissing my cat with a sick smile and wave to me. Sometimes she would come out and stand in front of my truck, so I couldn't leave and try to get me to fight her in front of my kids.

There were many times I just wanted to go ham and run her over just to be done with all of this, but instead, I would put my hands behind my back, holding my wrist with a tight grip because I knew I was a loose cannon at that point, and I would kill her in front of my kids if I let go. Honestly, the thought of killing her and losing what I had left of my shitty joke of a life crossed my mind many times, and the only thing that stopped me was what it would do to my kids. Because, at that point, my kids were the only reason for my living.

And as far as I'm concerned, my ex was just as guilty of creating extreme mental and emotional damage on my kids as she was. They were a tag team.

They kept my kids from me for so long that I wound up giving my ex-husband the bedroom furniture I had bought for them because it was just sitting at my brand new, four-bedroom home without them in it. And it wasn't beneath him to come with a Uhaul and a smirk to pick it all up. I wasn't giving up, but I thought at one point that giving in and being submissive was my only other option.

Every time I had a chance to see my kids, I would either try and take them to see my mother and stepfather in Delaware, or I would get the credit card out and take them somewhere to have fun because I had about seven hours to spend with them and driving up and back home consumed four of those seven hours. Going to my mother's wasn't always the best solution because I had to keep asking that they not speak using racial terms in front of my kids. We would sit down to eat dinner, and my stepfather would ask Mammy about school, and she would talk about a little boy she liked back then. If he had a name like Hector or Jesus, my stepfather would get upset, and he and my mother would dive in, telling her they didn't want her to be with a dirty spick or worse.

After a while, the kids were not too interested in going there anymore, as all we really did was sit around. It seemed I had a lot of rules for The Parents in their own homes, but it was simple, really; I didn't want them teaching my kids the things I was taught. And after a few years of random visits there, my mother made it clear that she wanted a call before I thought of visiting them in the future, which is fair. So, it wasn't too long before we stopped visiting altogether.

It didn't take much time for the costs of gas, tolls, and excursions to start racking up, and shortly I had accumulated roughly thirty thousand dollars in credit card debt, but I didn't care. All I cared about was seeing my kids and making that time great for them. I hoped that their memories with me would stick and somehow erase the hell they were dealing with, but they didn't.

And it didn't seem to matter because by then, I had become more and more depressed to the point where I couldn't work, which ultimately meant I couldn't pay my mortgage or bills. I was so afraid of what would happen to me and how I was going to survive. I was never really worried about surviving before I had kids, and I thought I was pretty good at it, but when you have to worry about someone else's life, everything changes. Suddenly, the things that used to matter to you just don't anymore. It's all about them. They didn't ask for this. They are completely innocent.

My mind and my body shut down again. I couldn't move, I couldn't function, and I couldn't work. And it didn't matter because all that was important to me was my time and relationship with my kids. I had always dealt with severe anxiety and depression, but as time went on, it became more difficult and more severe to the point where medication did not have its effect anymore.

The people I had worked with prior kept telling me that if I missed one mortgage payment, my house would go into foreclosure. I didn't have a fucking clue what that even meant, but I was afraid. I was stressed because my dad had cosigned for me, so I called my stepmom Diana to discuss the best way to tell him that I needed his help. I feared him, but I still needed help. She tried to soften the blow, but instead of my dad having a conversation with me or helping me try to figure something out, he called me and said,

"If you lose that house, I will get a rifle, come over there and stand at your doorway and blow your fucking brains out."

What is it with the men my mother chose and the threats of shooting her kids with a rifle?

Well, I guess I must have been a real pain in the ass to him? Truthfully, I always lived in fear, and I was sick of it, but I still just took the ride because that's all I knew. The only thing that kept me sane was knowing that I had to stay strong for my kids and the idea that my ex and his evil side piece would be stuck with each other for the rest of their lives. They deserve that much! Kinda a sick way of thinking, but it's how I felt at the time. When all was said and done, I left the house and moved once again.

"It's such a sickening feeling right now as I write this out. I still can't believe how brainwashed I was into thinking any of this was normal. There is so much I must leave out only because this would be longer than the Bible, and I'm nauseated enough.

I want to make something clear here. When I say, "It's all I knew," I'm not saying I didn't know there are always options in everything we do. I had ideas of what would be better, but I was afraid to cross those bridges because I didn't have support or someone coaching me through any of this. I think people get very comfortable in abusive situations, and stepping outside of the box is scary. Fear can be crippling. So, we stick to what we know. Yes, if I could go back in time, I would have done many things differently. I've learned a lot of lessons the hard way.

When all was said and done, I convinced myself that I had to pack and leave once again, and I did. I rented a small three-bedroom place, as I always did, with the hopes that my children would be able to stay. My life was in storage, and I fought to get back into my music career. I thought doing that would help get my mental state and shit together, so I started another cover band, contacted my booking agent, and got back to being me. It felt good to finally be on stage and sing again. The one place that always made me feel good and happy was on stage.

I was doing really well but found myself drinking a lot after work to numb my thoughts, erase my pain, and hopefully sleep one night. I knew drinking wasn't the answer, but I didn't care. Still, every morning I woke up with the same thoughts and feelings torturing me. After about a year or so, I had enough of the people I was around and needed to get out of there and climb another mountain, as my journey was not over yet.

A few months later, we finally had our custody court date. I felt pretty confident that I was good to go since I had a lawyer, but there was something about her that I couldn't put down. She made it very clear to me when I first started working for her that she was a lesbian. I wasn't sure why she felt the need to tell me this since I don't walk around telling everyone that I'm heterosexual, but I just figured that was her deal. She also started inviting me to her house to meet her friends often, which I didn't really think anything of at the time.

When I arrived at court, I was nervous yet hopeful. I heard my kids running in as they called for me, but when I turned around, Roman told them to stay away from me, so there was an issue at that point. I walked over and hugged my kids as Roman stood over me as if to chaperone the situation.

My Mammy asked me to take her to the bathroom, so Roman followed us, saying, "I have to take you guys downstairs. You can't be here." But my kids ignored her. As Mammy and I were in the lady's room, Roman opened the door, so she could get her last comment in. I, too, ignored her. I was too nervous about dealing with her bs, and I was excited at the same time because I hadn't seen my kids in weeks. Apparently, Gordon and Roman kept them from me to coach them for this court hearing in case they had to speak to the Judge.

Before the judge came in, my lawyer sat down next to me to tell me that she could not represent me. WHAT?!!!! She said this was out of her wheelhouse, and she legally couldn't do anything, and that she needed me to sign off to relieve her. I wonder in the back of my mind if she was paid off because I had been working for her through a trade for over 4 months, so why all of a sudden is she backing out? I thought to myself, are you fucking kidding me? Is this really happening to me right now? Why the F did you wait until now to tell me this?

But she didn't back off from her request. I had no idea what to do. I thought that I had to represent myself. I know now that I should have asked the judge to reschedule, but I was so nervous and afraid that, somehow, he would deny my request.

I signed off and cried silently. The judge walked in, all rise, and then the zoo arrived. Gordon, Roman, and their lawyer, whom Gordon had been doing credit card processing with for a few years. They all just sat there smiling, breaking their necks to look back at me. It was nauseating, to say the very least.

Judge Thomas was an absolute prick, and as much as I'm working on being my best, I still hope that one day he gets to feel what I felt the day he ripped my children from me. During the hearing, I answered whatever I had to and tried to give one-word responses, but the questions they came up with were absurd. They even printed 8x10 color photos of me from a photo shoot I had done for a nightlife magazine the year prior, which Gordon took me to. They held the pictures up of me in my bathing suit, asking, "Is this the kind of mother we want raising our kids?"

They actually made it seem like it was pornography, and the messed-up thing is that if I was fat and unhealthy, those pictures wouldn't have made a difference. If anything, one would think, yeah, well, she's in great shape, and obviously, she takes care of herself, so why wouldn't she be a good mother? Or what does any of this have to do with parenting?

That's just one of life's many BS hypocrisies. If you're fat, you can talk shit about someone who is skinny, but if you're skinny and tell someone they are fat, you are judging or racist or whatever the newest terms are nowadays. Either way, my pictures were a big deal, and mothers shouldn't wear bikinis. They should all just dress down, cut their hair short, and wear no makeup. Slum it. When it was my time, I did the best I could, but I wasn't prepared, and the judge mocked me many times. The whole thing was a cruel joke.

When all was said and done, the judge spoke to my kids and asked if they wanted to be with me. They said yes. He then asked if they wanted to be with their father, and they said yes. The judge determined that my kids loved both their parents. WOW! Then he decided that it was best not to uproot our kids as they were just recently registered by their father and Roman in a different school. He didn't determine that we were all abused or that Gordon had just met Roman not months before he moved our kids into her home. He didn't determine that since I had a brand new 4-bedroom home for my kids in their neighborhood that it would make the most sense or the fact that my kids were living with me the entire time after the divorce.

I saw that judge joke with Gordon's lawyer during the break as I sat in the courtroom alone the entire time. They were talking about golf and the bullshit they do when they hang out. What a joke and a disaster for my kids and me. We still got joint custody, but I received a bogus visitation schedule that was interfered with every single time by Gordon and Roman. They did everything they could to make the next 12 years a fucking nightmare for all of us. Man, the energy those two put into destroying our lives is incredible. And all for what? To be right, to look good to their friends, and to feel like they were in control. Seems pretty out of control to me, but they convinced anyone who would listen that I didn't want my kids and that I was a horrible person.

When I walked out of the courtroom, I was worn out, broken down, and just disgusted. I saw my kids, and they ran over to me to give me a hug as they cried and told me they wanted to go home with me. Roman made her way over and whispered to me, "Awe, poor Suzy didn't get her kids." I stood up and lunged at her. I didn't care anymore as I had nothing to lose, but my kids were watching. I told her she was a fucking whore, and I hope she fucking dies. Yeah, I know, not the nicest thing to say but at the time, that was all I could come up with.

My body was shaking, and my mind was fried. Security guards started walking up to us and told me they would have to detain me if I didn't leave, so I kissed my kids goodbye again and made my way to the car. It was one of the worse days of my life. I don't even remember what I did or how I got home, but I know I shut down for many weeks after and cried hysterically.

In my opinion, the court system is a bunch of crap! It's all about the money and who you know, and I was never one to bribe or schmoozz anyone to get ahead or to take a shortcut, so when I see that stuff happening right in front of me, it makes me see the world in a bad way. I know now that the only thing that matters in my world is what I am doing, how I feel about everything, and how I treat others. That doesn't mean I don't thoroughly despise all who were involved and wish they felt what I felt.

It means that I'm a work in progress, and it's important to me that I try and do my very best.

In 2010 I experimented with online dating. This was not something I had done before or felt comfortable with, but it seemed the way of the world now. I went back and forth for a while interviewing different candidates and really was not having the best of luck, but one did stand out of the crowd and seemed like he had his shit together. His resume consisted of him being the quarterback and, graduating from Temple University, working as an underwriter for a name-brand bank. He was a year older than me and had his own place, which at the time to me, was a big deal. He seemed established and a nice guy.

"Red Flag," if it seems too good to be true, it is! I fell once again for a book of lies and wound up in another situation with someone who had a major drug issue. He was a cheater, a liar, and a thief, and he lived a lot of his life in rehab centers. Of course, I had no idea, but I was about to find out and take yet another ride to the dark side.

The first night out to dinner seemed good. The conversation went well, and he went out of his way to compliment me. He wasn't really all that good-looking or my type, but I figured he had a nice personality and good credentials, which were a first for me, so why not. I'll name him Shark. Shark was about 6' tall, had brown hair, with eerie brown, bulgy devil eyes, and was in decent shape. I had never dated a German guy before, but I figured why not go outside of the box? I wasn't really feeling anything weird about him at all until the waitress came over to our table. He was very nice to her and seemed overly excited about her arm sleeves. She had a ton of ink up and down her arms, filled with the artwork of a famous artist that she undoubtedly loved.

I thought it was strange that he told her he would be right back as he ran to his car and returned with a couple of authentic paintings rolled up of that same artist. He gave them to her, almost relieved to get rid of them. She was shocked and extremely happy, as though they were expensive and hard to obtain.

Of course, I thought that it was really nice of him to be so generous. Funny enough, months later, I found out that he had stolen those expensive paintings from his ex-girlfriend. No wonder he seemed relieved to donate them. The sick thing is that I remember how empowered he seemed when giving them to her as if he was such a great guy. But at the time, I had no idea that they weren't even his to give.

A few minutes later, I heard music in the background and found one of my old bass players upstairs performing.

Looking back on this now, I realize that it was no coincidence that this particular friend, one of my old bass players, was at one time a major heroin addict, but not the first one I'd ever encountered and apparently not my last.

I couldn't believe it, and when he saw me, he grabbed his mic and made a point to tell everyone who I was and asked me to come up on stage to sing Bobby McGee, one of my favorite songs to sing. I was thinking, "How cool is this? I get to sing in front of my date. Surely he will be impressed."

Much to my surprise, his response wasn't too great. He told me I sounded good, then made a point to tell me he always hated that song. WOMP! For a few weeks, we went out to nice restaurants, and he took me to a few fun events. He really made a point to compliment me and introduce me to his friends and his kids, and eventually asked me to move in with him. I thought this was going somewhere. After all, I liked him, he had his shit together, and he introduced me to his kids, right? At the time, I had been traveling over an hour back and forth, so it seemed like a good plan.

But after about three weeks, something was fishy. I noticed that his friends who lived right behind him suddenly stopped all communication. When I asked why he just said there was a misunderstanding. I couldn't put it down though, and I started paying better attention to what was going on around me.

As the days went by, Shark became very sick. He would lie in bed for seven days at a time, only to come out for food and to use the bathroom. He'd pass me by in the hallway like I wasn't even there, and when I asked if he was ok, he would give me short snappy responses. I didn't have a good feeling about this, and something told me to go to the neighbors and find out what the deal was, so I did. His friends sat me down and explained that he was a heroin addict.

"What, get the F outa here. He doesn't use needles."

That was the day I realized that you could snort that shit. Then they told me he had stolen their credit cards, and they were filing charges. They warned me that he would ruin my life and that I wouldn't be the first woman he did that to.

The blood drained slowly from my head to my feet. Is this really happening? I didn't tell him I knew this because, apparently, he was dope sick, another term I learned that day. I didn't know his friends that well, so I wasn't sure if I believed them or not as they also told me that they were using along with him, and there was a part of me that didn't know if they were lying. In my experience with heroin addicts, they all lie. I figured I would find out for myself, and my antennas were up. I started going through his pictures and personal things while he was out for the count and found many photos of a beautiful brunette woman that I knew nothing of.

I was clear that we had not been together long enough for him to tell me about any of his past relationships, but I was curious for sure. I let everything go and decided to see what tomorrow would bring and not lose my shit. CONDITIONING!!!! It was all right in front of me, and I still chose not to see it!

Over time his behavior became routine. He would be good for a week, then dope sick the following week. I kept thinking, is this really my life? Friday nights were wasted. Saturday nights are wasted. This week and the next will be a waste. In the meantime, I got a call to audition for someone else's band and got the gig, so that kept me busy with weekly rehearsals and weekend gigs. I had also started working at a local gym as a personal trainer, so my days were filled.

Shark would attempt to attend my rehearsals and gigs, but thankfully he was too out of it to come to them all. I think the fact that I was out working at night sort of motivated him to try and stay clean for a day or two, but it didn't last, and he started to show an arrogant side which, on top of the "dope sickness," was a complete turnoff. I still hung around because

I really didn't want to move again and figured we would just be roommates; I really didn't care anymore. I decided to call him out on the dope thing and tell him I knew about him stealing his friend's credit card. He denied it all and made me believe that I was nuts.

One would think I'd be used to narcissism after my marriage of eleven years to the biggest narcissist in the world. But that clearly wasn't the case. Narcissists prey on insecure, broken people. And Shark hit the jackpot as I was as insecure and broken as they come. He would constantly compliment me and then break me down by picking me apart. How I did my hair, how I should wear my makeup and dress. I needed to shave my nose hair because it was more attractive. I needed to work out my calves. Even though I looked great, my calves were cankles. I would look better with extensions in my hair, and the list went on and on. Build her up, break her down. He was a master at it, and I guess I was the perfect puppet for his show.

Eventually, he would get sicker and sicker, and though he denied using, I found myself coming home from work and walking subconsciously into the bathroom to start a search. I would stand on the toilet seat and reach over the medicine cabinet. I have no idea why I did, but I did and found about fourteen tiny stamp-size blue bags that had weird names on them. WTF is this?

I confirmed from an old friend that it was indeed heroin. I confronted Shark, and he denied it. This went on for months, and I still found myself randomly finding dope in the weirdest places. I think the more interesting part was the fact that I would just get a message in my head to go into the closet, top shelf between his jeans, and WALLA, twenty bags of dope. Or to the back of the closet, I'd randomly check the inside pocket of an old suit covered in plastic. WALLA, seventeen bags of dope. What did I do? I flushed them all!

I'm sure you know what comes next. Shark lost his shit, and without saying it clearly, "Hey, did you take my dope?" He would start this weird dance, moving in circles, talking to himself, making weird loud yelp noises, pacing, and pacing the apartment until he mustered up the guts to calmly say,

"Did you take something? I need it back. It's not mine."

"What your dope I asked, did I take your dope? Well, I didn't take it per se. I flushed it."

Did you ever see a grown-ass man spin in place, moaning like a wounded animal, panting as if his best friend died or as if he was about to die? I did, and I have to say that though it was sad, it was pretty comical as well. I guess grab a laugh whenever you can. Do I have empathy now, yes? Did I have empathy, then? Absolutely not! I was completely disgusted, and the lies got bigger and bigger. And I still stayed because I didn't have the energy to move again.

Of course, he wanted me to come clean (haha) and tell him that I was lying, and it was right here, but it wasn't. I flushed it. I guess I'm lucky he didn't lose his mind and attack me. He just made some phone calls and left for a few hours. When he returned, I would be gone, and when I returned, he would be high. A while later, Shark came up with this great idea to get a kitten. I suppose to keep me there. The kitten was dead the next morning. He decided to get two more kittens, and well, it was the same deal. In two months' time, he managed to accumulate nine kittens, and they all died. I found one with its head stuck between the wall on top of the dryer.

That was horrible! I accused him of doing the unthinkable because I heard one kitten crying in the bathroom while he was supposedly clipping its claws. None of this made sense to me because the kitten was only a few weeks old and barely had claws. He was horrified that I would even think that he would give a tiny kitten heroin, but I watched that tiny new healthy kitten walked sideways and fall over only to be found dead the next morning, sooooo I wasn't convinced. Shark is the only one who knows the truth if he even remembers.

I let him know I was done with the kittens. Imagine telling your kids every week that the new kitten from last week died just like the one from last week and the week before. If I was traumatized, then what were they thinking? What were they feeling?

We went food shopping one day, and out of nowhere, two cops followed us out to our car, asking for his ID. WTF is going on now? "Oh, it's nothing, baby doll (ugh, I'm cringing). It was a misunderstanding." A few days later, the FBI came to the house. WTF? As I hid behind the door in the back bedroom, not making a move and trying to listen, all I could hear was my heart pounding. My face felt like it was on fire, my hands sweaty, and my body shook while I overheard them discussing Shark stealing his uncle's dead wife's wedding ring and other jewelry. The funny thing is that the week before he brought me to meet his uncle, he randomly mentioned there was a door in his uncle's house that was never locked.

I wanted to vomit, but again, it was all a misunderstanding and nothing to worry about. In the meantime, the court notice for the credit card Shark didn't steal arrived. The police obtained video footage from the food store of him using their credit card to buy fruit and protein powder. In the back of my mind, I recalled watching Shark act funny in the food store. Out of the corner of my eye, I noticed him being shifty and watched him steal vitamins, but I never said anything because I knew he would just do his weird dance and tell me that I hurt his feelings for even thinking such a thing.

Even though all the signs and proof were right in front of me, he convinced me somehow that it was all a big misunderstanding and apologized for the embarrassment. I realized that the same day he was accused of stealing his friend's credit card, he had filled up my gas tank and paid for his dry cleaning with that same credit card. A week or so after, I reluctantly went to the court hearing with him. But when I saw his friends there and the anger and disappointment in their eyes, I was mortified and felt like a complete loser.

Later on, I found about thirty more bags of dope and witnessed him nodding off as he tried to stay alert so I wouldn't leave. I dumped them too, and after hours of dancing and losing his shit, he finally agreed to go to a rehab facility for about three months.

Relief! I was willing to stick around if he was willing to get help. After all, he was the best of the worst of the losers I'd dated in the past, right? That makes sense, right? NAW!!! I found myself counting down the days until he would leave. To be clear, this was not a romantic relationship by any means. In fact, there wasn't any intimacy after week one because his girlfriend, heroin, was his number one priority, and anyone who knows her knows that she doesn't allow certain body parts to function at all when she is around. I clearly didn't want to move at this time, nor did I want to be around this human with drug issues, so I'd spend hours and hours in my truck after work parked at the shopping center alone. I didn't want to go back there and deal with yet another shitty situation.

Have I mentioned yet that I hated my fucking life?

Have I mentioned yet that words cannot express the sickening feeling I had in the pit of my stomach every single day? I never felt more alone. Of course, having this destitute mindset, I attracted drug addicts and narcissists, cheaters, and liars, people whose lives were way worse than mine and were past the point of acting human. But it was all I knew. I thought I could help them or change them even though I wasn't right in the head, not realizing yet that I was the one who needed to change in order to have the life that I deserved.

At this point, I was struggling, but I truly wanted to be alone. It's interesting to me to realize how I slowly fell down a rabbit hole a little bit each day, each moment, and then all of a sudden, I was at the bottom, and I still couldn't fully process how I landed there or what to do. It was like I was trapped in a tiny box filled with fear, anxiety, and lies and surrounded by probably some of the nastiest humans, but I didn't see it at the time. I was a walking zombie.

My energy field had so many holes in it that there was no way I could attract anyone or anything meaningful in my life. My environment was a prison. I just sucked in all the low-riders. And really, who wants to deal with that shit? So, I pretty much lost any and all connections I had left of any good humans. I'm pretty sure when my number came up on the phone, there was a lotta swiping going on!

My good friend, Maria from high school, was the only friend I had left at the time, and unfortunately, she knew all too well what living with an addict was all about. She spent many hours on the phone with me playing devil's advocate and trying to soothe me. But in time, I realized that the only person who could save me was me.

The time had come when Shark would return from rehab, and things seemed ok for about a minute. :/ He got a new underwriting gig making around 90k, and he was ready to start his new clean life. But in less than two weeks, all the same shit started happening again. Here comes the new show! I guess in his mind, in order to make me believe he was getting himself together, he needed to demonstrate a new routine. He would pack a lunch at night, pull out a suit for the next day, shower in the morning at 6 am, get dressed, and go to work.

I really thought he was doing well, although there were still small signs of something being off. This was about the 9th new job he had. My practical mind couldn't fathom how any bank would hire him after losing so much work time and having so many new jobs in such a short period of time. I just thought he was either really good at his job or a really good resume writer. And I believed that he was going to work every day. He would even tell me he was going to the bank each week to deposit his paycheck.

Something just wasn't right in the air. My kids were over for the day, as I stopped bringing them there when Shark was around. My son Bamm handed me a letter that bothered him. It was a letter to a bank stating that he, loser #3, was sorry to announce he had pancreatic cancer and that he would have to travel out of the country to seek a new treatment and wouldn't know when he was to return. OMG!!! I told my son not to worry, and it wasn't true. I really didn't have words at this point. I just knew to keep my eyes open for the next bullshit event that was to come. And I decided not to let on that I found this letter.

For about two weeks, Shark would come home at 5 pm and get changed like nothing ever happened. In the meantime, I was having issues with my computer and had to figure out what the hell was going on because my life was on that thing. I started getting viruses on my computer, bad ones. I would spend endless amounts of time figuring out how to flush them and clean my system. I got really serious about backing up my files, thinking there was something wrong with my computer, until a thought came to me to check my history. My inner guide at work again without me knowing it.

I found porn in my history and got this sick feeling in my gut. In a nutshell, I accused him of watching porn on my computer, but of course, he denied it and suggested that it could have been my children. At that point, I wanted to stab him! JK I couldn't figure out how he would be using my computer while we were both at work during the day.

I wound up losing any tiny amount of trust I could muster up for him and uploaded some really good spyware. Anytime anyone typed anything on my computer, I could see it. URLs, usernames, passwords, emails, anything! I could log on from any device and see it all. I chose to announce this to everyone,

I guess, as a warning, but that didn't matter. I waited a few days and then logged in. Whoa! And here we go! Was he watching porn on my computer? Yep, for sure, no doubt, there it was right in front of me, time-stamped, location, website addresses, etc. And much to my surprise, there were a bunch of emails to someone unknown to me.

"Dear "other woman," I'm sorry I had to cancel our dinner plans last Friday. Unfortunately, I was called to Germany to sit with my dying grandmother last minute. I'm not sure how long I will be out of the country, but I will try to reconnect with you when I return." WOW! Ok, it's confirmed. I'm a complete asshole. I wasn't even hurt by this; I was nauseous, and I wanted to immediately confront this MF'er, but as I walked into the other room, I noticed that my handbag was disheveled. I mean, my things were literally hanging out of it, which answered the question I had about why I heard him stumble abruptly when I was walking into the room.

I immediately went into my purse and saw that my credit card was missing. Shark didn't know that I had set him up, but I did. I had a feeling he was going to try and steal it, so I left it in a special spot so I would notice if it was missing, and I did. I had to stop and breathe. I had to sort this all out and be specific with my words. Which would I confront him about first? The porn, the girlfriend, or taking my credit card. I figured the credit card was most important, so that's where I started. I walked up to him, stuck my hand out, and said,

"Give me my credit card, now!"

Lo and behold, he was in disbelief, and a face of shock and wonder appeared.

"I repeat, give me my fucking credit card now!"

Of course, he had no idea what I was talking about. He would never steal my credit card. This went on for about ten minutes until I told him to hand it over or I would call the police. I actually felt bad that he was high and not on his game. I got to him when he was weak and stupid, which was probably a good thing. He handed it to me, saying,

"Here, I did this for us!"

Again WOOOOOOW!

"I did this so we could start cleaning up our finances."

I had to step back from either knocking him out or laughing hysterically. "You did this for us. You were worried about our finances?" Luckily, I learned at least one big lesson from my ex-husband about combining finances so I would never attach my money to his. I confronted him after that about the emails, Germany, and the porn, which only led to his stupid drug dance and me being completely annoyed. I told him I was done! Later that night, he got high again and was in bed for about two weeks. I grabbed a few things and went to the gym. I'd rather sleep on the floor of my office than return there and figured I'd get the rest later.

I had a few gigs coming up with my band, so there was something to focus on, but eventually, he showed up at a gig without my knowing, and things were weird.

I lost my voice!

I think the last straw for me was on stage in February of 2011, singing my heart out with a mediocre cover band, and I literally lost my voice on stage. I remember the guitar player looking at me like I had just murdered someone.

"Is your mic on?"

"WHAT?!!!"

So now, after losing everything I had, my kids, my marriage, my house, my dignity, I lost the only thing I had left, my voice, my money maker, my identity, my dreams, my life. I couldn't talk, and I could barely whisper.

I had been to five different ENT specialists without any relief. None of them could find anything, but it made no sense to me because I couldn't even talk.

After months of not being able to speak or sing, I stopped listening to music because it broke my heart to hear the squeaky, horrible sounds coming from my voice box. I stopped talking and only whispered. I lost all of my contacts in the club scene and had to figure out, while at my lowest of lows, how to make money again.

As my daughter would say right now, "I'm dead, YO." My son would say, "WOMP."

Once again, I had to start over. I was always into fitness and had a personal training business after taking a few health and fitness courses. And I started competing in powerlifting for a short period of time. I had a lot of different jobs over the years, probably more than living situations. It was my way of surviving the boredom of staying in one place too long. It took every ounce of energy I had to wake up each day and do what I needed to do to survive. I felt like a complete loser. I had no one, my insides were raw, my heart was broken, I missed my kids desperately, my friends and family turned on me, and I was homeless again at forty-one, sleeping in hotels or on the office floor at my gym.

I hated my life, my heart ached for my kids, and I literally lost my voice and what I thought back then was my entire identity.

In 2012 I had started training for a bodybuilding competition twice a day, seven days a week. I figured six months was enough time to transition and clear my head by focusing on something that would be a big challenge for me. I also started documenting my training and results on FakeBook daily. For some reason, this disturbed my brother D and my family. D made that quite apparent by messaging me on Fakebook, telling me I should be ashamed of myself and that I should stop working out and spend time with my kids.

Unfortunately, he was buddies with my ex-husband Gordon, and believed the brainwashing he was being fed. I had asked him if I should stop living too, because he believed what my ex was telling him. I was pretty disappointed in my brother and the lack of support, but he was too busy being sucked into the hoax, just like everyone else. I'd like to say that I wasn't surprised, but in all honesty, I was upset and angry with him. To this day, we do not speak. I did reach out to him when he was facing the tragedy of his only son passing at a very young age, but he was non-respondent.

It was quite apparent that no one believed my side of the story, not even my family. And they all totally supported my ex and his girlfriend's accusations that I left my kids on his girlfriend's doorstep, never to return. This was heartbreaking for me, but it also gave me the strength to focus on doing something for myself. I needed a challenge so badly, and it physically hurt to breathe. I put my blinders on and went full force into my workouts. I hated my brother and everyone, for that matter, for not believing me, but I knew that I wasn't up for trying to convince anyone anymore. My side of the story didn't matter, and I didn't have it in me, nor did I want to care what anyone thought of me ever again. I was done with everyone!

It was show-time, and I did what I had to do. There were some glitches, like the music stopping during my not-so-polished routine. I had no idea what I was doing, but I did it. It wasn't graceful, but I did it. I won first place in my weight class. No one in my family showed up to support me, but I still did it! The cool thing was how many people on social media supported and were happy for me when I announced at the competition that I had won. It really made me feel good for about a minute. And that one minute gave me the strength to get to the next.

June 2012, Miss PA

About three weeks after I left the apartment, Shark's sister called me. She was concerned that she hadn't heard from him in a while. I had only met his sister twice and couldn't believe that they had the same parents as she really had her life together and was very nice to me. I took a leap and decided to tell her everything about the heroin and that she should be concerned. She lived in New York, so I offered to go over that day and check to make sure he was ok and update her.

As I entered the house, I found garbage everywhere, dirty plates lying around, and old food in the sink. The smell was awful, the bathroom was filthy, and his bedroom door was locked. I worried for a second that he might be dead, and TBH, at the same time, I felt some relief. After banging on the door, he finally answered, and he was dope sick again. This time was the worse I'd ever seen him.

I told him his family was worried about him, but he was out of it and didn't seem to care. I told him that his family offered to send him to another very expensive rehab costing over sixty grand in another state, where he was to stay for six months. He agreed and made that move.

I don't even want to get into the rest of it because it makes me physically ill, but when all was said and done, he broke out early, essentially screwing his family over financially, and started using once again within about a week. I'll end this story because the bottom line now is that I made it out safe and alive. I did see Shark's face, sunken down in shame once about a year or so later as he walked into the gym with his new girlfriend he had met at rehab. These stories are still sensitive for me to discuss, but I am working on not holding myself hostage anymore.

CHAPTER 17 | STARTING OVER AGAIN

Move number 49 or 50 into a beautiful home with a lady named Annie, who was looking for a roommate. Annie was about 10 years older than me and very nice. She had the entire bottom floor of her house empty, just waiting for someone to occupy it. It was perfect for my kids and for me when they were "allowed" to stay over once. :/

This move was the beginning of a new chapter and my entirely different life moving forward. I just didn't know it yet. I had spent so much time alone, and I didn't care about anything anymore. I was angry, afraid, alone, and contemplating a move to another country where I would just start over and even change my name.

At least that thought had crossed my mind, but I knew that I would be taking myself with me. Like Linus from Charlie Brown, I'd be forever dragging my dirty blanket everywhere until I committed to completely changing. I felt bad because Annie wanted to hang out and be a girlfriend as she tried daily to visit me and talk, but I was completely shut down and the only thing I had wanted was to be alone. I didn't have the energy to explain anything.

One night, around my birthday, in January of 2013, my body was dealing with bronchitis for 14 days, and I felt horrible! I was tired of laying around feeling like shit, so I reluctantly put a CD on, as in some moments, the silence and being alone were all I could hear. It was an Adel song, and within seconds, I was in tears. It was incredibly depressing, as I related to it all too well. It wouldn't have been the first time I dropped to my knees, bawling my eyes out. I had this hardcore victim mentality, and the fact that I couldn't sing those songs, or any song anymore, was brutal! :/

Then, in the next moment, it all clicked for me; I was alone again.

As crazy as it sounds, I abruptly stopped, and kind of stepped outside of myself and everything around me. I knew that blaming everyone else for what I had been through got me zero, so I stopped beating that drum.

Out of nowhere, a clear message came to me, and I decided to change my entire life and personality. I remembered that this was my show, and I was in full control of what I did and how I handled things. A concept that I believed and obviously forgot to apply. I heard a clear voice in my mind saying, "You have to change now, not later. Change now!" Over and over again, change, change! At first, I thought I was losing my mind, but after having many transcendental experiences, I figured I was connecting to something higher and more powerful than me. So I decided to finally listen.

The thoughts of being with my children, having a big, beautiful home again, and being successful financially again, were flowing through me. Just breaking free of the chains of the past and the anger I had built up inside me for so many years. There were so many visions and thoughts I had to put it all to paper.

It was the first time my mind started working for me instead of against me. All of the thoughts and signs screamed, "Change now." As I recall all of this, it was quite amazing indeed. My mission was beginning with or without me. And the idea of living another forty-five years doing the same things over and over would be the biggest mistake I could ever make. I quickly took my journal out, gathered my emotions, and with a still mind, I started writing, **"Do the complete opposite of everything you have ever done in the past that didn't serve you."**

I made a detailed list of what I wanted in life and what I didn't want. A list of the types of relationships I deserved, what was acceptable and not acceptable. I made a list of what I wanted in a romantic partner and what I wouldn't put up with. There was a list of how I wanted to be treated and what was not happening ever again. How I would walk, how I would talk, how I wanted my body to look. I wrote down my dreams, my goals, and where I saw myself in ten years. I listed everyone in my life who was good for me and a list of anyone who had a negative impact on me, that talked down to me, judged me, etc., and decided that they needed to be exed out of my energy field.

That was easy. Most of those people were my family members and my friends. Pretty much left me at ground zero, but I didn't care.

There was something inside me that knew this was the right path to take, and if I didn't take it, I would wind up like the people I didn't admire. The Parents, the people I saw around me who retired, grew old, and laid around waiting to die while taking prescription medications and watching the news all day. I wanted so much more. I wanted to be remembered for my accomplishments, I wanted to travel and see the world, and I wanted to be a rockstar. I had a deep feeling that my voice would come back, but I would be using it in a different way.

I committed to journaling daily again, something I had done for years as a kid and into my adult years. I lived in silence when I was home from work. No TV, which I rarely watched anyway, no radio, no phone calls unless it was my children or one of the three friends, I thought I had left. I started reading daily again. I was always big into buying self-help books, reading some of them, and putting them down only to collect dust because I didn't have any focus. I would read a paragraph and have no idea of what I just read, then get discouraged and place the book next to all the other books I never finished and always felt defeated. At one point, I believed I had dyslexia, yet I could read and write anything backward like a pro.

I could read for ten minutes and pass out sleeping. It was frustrating. But I was obsessed with change. So now, every book I read, I would read out loud. It was a great idea because it forced me to stay conscious.

I am big into The Law of Attraction, mindfulness, and the science of the mind-body connection. I started studying, listening to lectures, and taking hard notes from well-known scientists, speakers, healers, and entrepreneurs, who practice and study The Quantum Field, Law of Attraction, Energy Healing, Meditation, Epigenetics, Mindfulness, Plant-based lifestyle, Fitness, Finances, and all that fall into those categories. Never in a million years would I believe that I'd be so excited about studying and learning any of this stuff. I started making charts and tacking them to my walls so they would be right in front of me. Since then, I have spent at least 50% of my days in the morning and after work, sleep, and social events, studying and rewiring my brain.

I didn't know what was going on, but it was like I was possessed and couldn't stop. I couldn't get enough, so I would listen repeatedly and jot down the main points that really stuck with me about strength and courage, change, and a higher power. This went on for months and months, and then I found information on the subconscious mind and the ego. Information about personality disorders not being an illness but a real crutch if they are not identified and nurtured, trapped energy for just about anyone with trauma. I loved the idea that I could pick apart and identify my different emotions and connect them with their individual personalities and traumas and work on them. Work on loving them and thanking them for protecting me all those years, then setting them free, as I develop new personalities.

Eventually, my walls were covered with poster boards and different statements of power and growth. I bought some new journals and got busy writing out what was going on in my head, pulling it all apart like a mad scientist to try and get to the root of why the first 45 years of my life were a complete disaster in every area. Don't get me wrong; I had a lot of successful situations for someone who had a highly dysfunctional family and lived out of boxes for a lot of years. But there was nothing so successful that I was proud to discuss with anyone other than my children, my businesses with friends, my singing, and my first big house that I helped the builders design.

I couldn't really be proud of all of that because everything was gone now. I was simply grateful that I made it this far and for the fact that I always found a way to make money to survive.

I wasn't really a TV person. The only time I watched a TV show was when my DVR was out of memory because I had so many recordings of General Hospital just waiting for me to binge-watch. That was something my Memom, and I watched when I was little, so I attached a lot of good memories of my time with her to it. Eventually, I started noticing that I had no interest in the drama of that show anymore and went cold turkey. I had anxiety watching which couple was having an affair or who killed who now. I really never concerned myself with needing to know the news because I've always felt that it was all negative and stressful. There was nothing about it that served me.

And I could care less about the weather. I would just simply open my front door or look out the window before I left the house, if I left it at all. A lot of my old friends would say, ***"You need to know what's going on in the world,"*** but I felt like there was no real reason for me to engage in anything that stressed me out. I'd rather bury my head in the sand.

Think about it, back when I was a kid in the early 70s, I didn't watch the news. I had no real insight into all the diseases and troubles of the world unless I was around adults who were obsessing about something. The only scary time I gave any of my attention to was 9-11. I was at work, and everyone was freaking out, so I drove home in a panic to get my kids out of school and in my arms. "If we're gonna die, we're gonna die together." And the second time I took notice of something newsworthy was covid 2020 when I observed the world panicking, taking sides, dividing, and freaking out with masks covering their faces up to their eyes.

And though this is not a popular belief amongst many, I wasn't worried about dying because I believe in my immune system more now than ever in my life.

I haven't had a science project injected into my body since I was a small child, and I don't plan on ever having one in the future. But the bottom line is I skated through that because I refused to watch the news. Let me stop on that note.

My obsession with the subconscious and conscious mind developed into me homeschooling myself for hours upon hours every day. Although I've stated a million times that I truly hated school when I was a kid, this was just different. These stellar human beings that I was mesmerized by were just fantastic teachers. I landed on each one of them at exactly the time when I was ready for a new chapter in my life.

"When the student is ready, the teacher will appear."

–Lau Tsu

Meditation is my thing now too. I have always been an on-and-off meditator, but I started practicing meditation again seven days a week. Sometimes I'd get up at 3 am and just meditate for an hour or two just because I felt like I was being called to do so. In the beginning, many years ago, I didn't have a strict routine, and I wasn't great at focusing. I also didn't know that "knowing thyself" means being aware and conscious of my thoughts, quieting my mind so that I can listen, or even slipping in there and reprogramming my subconscious mind to be exactly who I want to be and erasing those old programs. Recognizing and overcoming the endless mind chatter, emotions, mindset, behavior patterns, and being a victim is crazy shit, exciting shit, phenomenal shit!

If you're reading this and enjoying it, I made a short list of the amazing humans whose work I've studied and continue to study in the order presented.

- **Tony Robbins:** (Unleash the power within, Money master the game, speaker, teacher)
- **Joel Olsteen:** (I am not religious, but I love his teachings)
- **Bishop TD Jakes:** (I love his teachings and powerful messages)
- **Markus Rothkranz:** (The Healthy Life, plant-based lifestyle, mindfulness, etc.)
- **John Rose:** (SFV - coached me through my first 30-day juice fast (solid food vacation)
- **Paul Manphilly:** (Coach in Big Money Investing) Changed my financial life.
- **Jon and Missy Butcher:** (Life Book) I Wrote my first Life Book in 2020.
- **Abraham Hicks:** (The Law of Attraction, with Ester Hicks, changed my life forever)
- **Melanie Beckler:** (Ask the angels) Beautiful soul, a great teacher.
- **Less Brown:** (Motivational speaker)
- **Joseph Rodrigues:** (Discussions and breakdowns of these same topics)
- **Eckhart Tolle:** (Awaken to a life of purpose and presence)

- **Dan Pena:** (The trillion-dollar man, great teacher, a little harsh but to the point)
- **Evan Carmichael:** (Rules for success, great work)
- **Tom Bilyeu:** (Impact Theory, interesting mind, great topics)
- **Lewis Howes:** (The school of greatness, great human with great topics)
- **Marissa Peer:** (Great speaker on Rapid Transformational Therapy)
- **Sadguru:** (Teachings of spirituality and yoga)
- **Teal Swan:** (Self-dev teacher, deep human, crazy smart, beautiful, and interesting)
- **Steve Harvey:** (Fav) (The King of real-life talk and experiences)
- **Dr. Bruce Lipton:** (Cellular biologist, teacher, author, and so on)
- **Dr. Joe Dispenza:** (Fav) (Becoming Supernatural, speaker, changing from the inside out)
- **Ed Mylett:** (Change - Max out, leadership journeys, business leader) Cool cat!
- **Gary Vee:** (Entrepreneur, coach, hardcore)
- **Alex Ferrair:** (Next Level Soul. NDE discussions. A must watch!)
- **My husband:** (Cheems - patience, kindness, generosity, and loyalty)

There are many more, of course, but these are the humans that guided me over the last 12 years in a lot of ways, so far, without knowing. I respect and cherish them all and their work. I've learned so much from these teachers and try to go back to each of them as I'm called. Once I got deeper into the matters of the mind, things really started to click for me. I took tons of notes day after day. I found that the practice of writing things out assisted in burning the info into my brain. Before all of this, I could memorize the lyrics and story of five songs a week but could not retain meaningful information. And the funny thing was I didn't mind writing and writing and writing. It still blows my mind as I am "writing this book."

In between all this drama and working on changing my life, I met someone who changed everything. In all honesty, we knew each other for years prior, but I wasn't looking, and he was in a relationship. It was as if he was a blur, a body without a face. His real name is Anthony/Tony, but I call him Cheems. I swore I'd never date another Italian guy, but I guess I was wrong. Cheems is about 5' 10" tall, has dark- thick and wavy hair and sparkly blue eyes, and Cheems is Italian. Cheems is a rare find, in my opinion.

My friend JJ at the time thought that we would be a great match. I didn't see it at all, as I never really considered anything like that, especially since Cheems had been married for about 25 years and has 2 grown kids. So, dating him was out of the question, but my friend JJ kept pushing. Cheems and I would normally say hi at the gym and maybe have a short conversation here and there over the years, but that was about it. And occasionally, I would send people his way for renovation jobs as he is a general contractor.

From what I understand from Cheems himself was that he was in a loveless marriage and incredibly unhappy. He said that he had planned to leave for years but committed to staying until his kids graduated college. He said he never spoke of this other than with his father, Augusto, who had passed many years ago. During many conversations, I encouraged Cheems to try and work things out as he had stayed this long. I figured there must be something there that he could spark, but he said he was done.

He told me that he did everything in his power to make the marriage work, but there was no changing the inevitable. Right around my birthday in January, Cheems and I started talking more and more. Not "talking" like the kids do today. We had meaningful conversations and grew our friendship more and more. I don't really know what happened other than we clicked, and he asked me if I would consider spending time with him. As much as I liked him, I didn't want that guilt or burden on me as far as dating a married man, even though he was very clear that he was leaving either way.

This was a particularly difficult situation for me because getting involved with a married man was not part of my plan, and it was not on my list of positive aspects of the relationship I wanted, if any. There is a lot of guilt that comes with this kind of involvement, not only in myself but from the other people involved. I told Cheems that I would not get into any situation with him until he presented separation papers to his wife at the time and made it clear to her that he was leaving. And he said he would. It took him some time because he worried about his kids rejecting him or hating him, but he said that he decided he wanted to know what it would be like to be happy.

I didn't tell too many people about this situation because I worried that I would be judged harshly, and most who knew said that he would never leave. I was just a side piece. But it wasn't like that at all. He was kind and thoughtful. We had great conversations that lasted hours. I trusted him completely. But like most divorces, his was drug out for a while, and Cheems didn't care how long it would take and went through it. He had to sell his many rental properties and his home, and he walked away with two contractor bags of clothes, his old beat-up work truck, and his tools. He lost everything and gained a ton of debt. But he didn't care. He just wanted to be happy.

At the time, he had no family as he expressed that his wife had forced him to eliminate all of them, his mother, brother, nieces, nephew, and every one of his friends. None of them fit her mold. He said it had been over twenty-two years since he last saw his mother, but at the time, keeping peace at his house was all he cared about. I had a hard time understanding why anyone would do something like this and a hard time understanding why Cheems didn't fight for his family, but he explained that it was just easier to go along with it to keep the peace. Cheems and I worked on contacting his family and friends. He was very hesitant to do so as he felt that none of them would ever forgive him or accept him after all the years he had been gone, but the opposite was true.

I started communicating with his friends and family, and to his surprise, everyone was waiting with open arms. They all seemed to understand and knew what he had been going through and graciously let it go. We visited so many people in such a short amount of time. It was sad and heartwarming altogether. I'll never forget the day I contacted his brother Gus and set up a surprise visit to see his mom, Rosina. Rosina, now in her late 80s and right off the boat, had no idea that she would see her first son again. She said she prayed to God every day for over twenty-two years that someone would wake her son up and take him away from the situation he was in, and she was in a lot of pain from her loss, but she had faith that God would come through.

The day we went to Rosina's house, she was in the kitchen of her tiny apartment in Philadelphia, cooking for her son Gus and her grandchildren. We walked in, and Cheems went up to her. Rosina stood there in disbelief as if she were paralyzed, then went in for the bear hug. It was such an emotional experience for all of us. I took out my phone and hit record to capture this amazing reunion of mother and son, and in the pit of my stomach, I could feel her heartache as, at that moment, I felt the loss of my children as well. There were so many tears at one time from everyone there. Tears were flying from Rosina and Cheems. I was crying, Gus was crying, and the kids were crying. I can't even explain how happy I was for everyone there.

Not too long after, I organized a catered 50th birthday party for Cheems in a beautiful hall. I invited all his friends and family. Out of fifty-two invites, fifty-one people showed up to see Cheems. The day of the party, we had a major snowstorm, the roads were blocked, and traffic was crazy, but just about everyone showed up. It was a little uncomfortable for me because there were so many people that I'd never met, and they all knew that Cheems had left the situation he was in and was with me at that point. But it went well, and everyone there who came to see him was happy for him and supportive.

Cheems is a rockstar in his own right. I never saw so many people love one guy, and it was genuine. To this day, every time we meet up with friends or family, Cheems is the center of attention, and everyone loves him. It can be quite annoying, lol.

That was nine years ago, and now we have such an amazing connection with his family, his friends, and mine as well. I never imagined something like this was even possible, but then again, there's not much that surprises me anymore.

Our relationship started out very slowly as we had little time to be together the first year, but the time we spent was genuine. We walked, talked, danced, and dreamed together as much as we could. Our conversations were deep, nothing like anything I had ever experienced.

I sat down one day journaling and decided to write a list of all of Cheems' positive aspects. He's handsome, kind, generous, brave, loving, caring, strong, honest, and patient. He's a hard worker and very meticulous in everything he does. He genuinely cares about people and his family. He is loyal to the ones he loves. He has all the qualities I've always wanted but could never find. Sometimes I wish it hadn't taken so long to meet him, but I'm eternally grateful that he was finally sent my way.

When I tell you I walked around in a bubble for years, I walked around in a bubble for many years. Cheems tells me that he dreamt of me his whole life. He just couldn't put a face to the soul. It was like we lived parallel lives. He grew up in Northeast Philly, and I grew up in Southwest Philly. We were around each other for years, five days a week, but I never really saw him.

I know now that, at the time, I wasn't ready or in the right state of mind for someone like him. My negativity and fear only attracted the low-level zombies. Cheems only appeared to me when I cleaned up my vibration, cleaned up my mind, and cleaned up my emotional state. After both of us retired from our "not-so-healthy relationships," we connected and started over together with nothing in the bank. He lost it all, and I lost it all. Over time, together, we managed to create a successful family business, and we are now very prosperous in everything we do.

He is more than a best friend to me; he has my heart, and I am so grateful that I changed my life because I would never have seen him the way I do now. And he undoubtedly would have never come to me when he did. After one year, Cheems and I went on a vacation to the Poconos, and he asked me to marry him. I accepted with zero doubt in my mind. It was the first and only time I was 100% sure of anything. I asked many times if he was sure he was ready to get into another commitment after being in such a long relationship prior, and he told me he had no doubts in his mind and didn't need to look any further.

Over the years, Cheems and I have only grown closer. Our relationship is tight, and we respect each other. We work together almost seven days a week with our business and get along great. We do not fight. We discuss. Yes, there were a few times we had to work the kinks out and got a little heated, but neither of us enjoyed yelling or fighting, so it worked out great. Together the sky is the limit for us, and we've grown to be very prosperous in our endeavors. We purposefully plan weekend getaways a few times a year and a few 2-week vacations to unwind. When we are away, our time together is very valuable, and it gives us uninterrupted time to reconnect.

There are many things I love about my Cheems, but I think the thing I love the most is how he supports me in every way. No matter what it is that I want to do, he will hear me out, discuss everything with me and simply support me through it all. When I told him I was writing this book, he never questioned a thing and asked what he could do to help. When I told him I wanted to invest in the stock market, he said OK, let's do it. When I told him I would take over the back end of his business, he said that would be great and never questioned what I was doing. I think the reason we get along so well is that we both want the same things in life. We want to be happy, have our family together, and make a difference in this world.

Every Wednesday night, Cheems and I shoot pool together. He calls it "shit talk Wednesday." I guess because we never really talk trash, and he likes to get all hype when he's playing. It's comical, to say the very least. Cheems is very good at pool and taught me how to play over the years. But he hasn't taught me how to beat him yet. We turn on our big JBL speakers and blast the music. He even bought two wireless microphones so we could sing. I didn't want to sing at first because I was afraid to make a fool of myself, but he continued to encourage me to try, and eventually, I got much better. I'm nowhere near the vocalist I once was, but I have my voice back, in more ways than one, and that's all that matters to me. It's kind of strange that he never got to see me sing or be in my element, but I understand that that's not who I am anymore.

Boy, I never thought I would say that and feel calm!

After our pool games, we retreat outback, where he has two big heat lamps set at full blast and a fat cigar. That's a guy thing! We have a few drinks, sit back, and together, we dream and talk about our future. Where we will go next, what our new house will look like, what kind of parties we will have and so on. We are cocreating at its best. We talk about our accomplishments and how far we've come from nothing. Sometimes I sit back and just listen to him talk and watch him dream. I look at his beautiful eyes and wonder how I ever got so lucky to be with such an amazing human being. I am grateful. When I look at him, I see the beautiful soul that resides in that perfect, chiseled body he has.

I feel like a teenager sometimes and get excited when he comes home. We have a very special and deeply connected relationship. I don't think there is anything I couldn't talk to him about, and he gives me his full attention. I think of him all day long. I dream of him. I love the way he smells, the way he kisses so passionately, and the way he loves all our children and me.

Cheems and I are different yet similar in a lot of ways. I still very much enjoy my alone time to write or read or meditate, and he enjoys his alone time too. I think it's very healthy to live in the same house with someone and have personal time to unwind or decompress after a long day. It's almost a relief not to have to worry about entertaining or making sure everything is alright if I'm not there. I love that I don't need to overthink things anymore or worry about him doing things that I had dealt with in the past through other situations.

We married on July 5th, 2016, in a small church in Bucks County, PA, on a Tuesday at 3:00 because that was the only time Cheems' best friend Mike could make it. Cheems wanted Mike to stand as his best man because he said that he wasn't allowed to have Mike at his first wedding, and that really seemed to upset him.

I'm not sure why we rushed it, but neither one of us wanted a grand ceremony. We didn't have enough time to tell everyone or plan, so Cheems suggested putting the info on Fakebook.

About 20 people showed which was more than either of us expected, and we headed over to a restaurant for a late lunch after. We had a nice time but not many good pictures, so we decided to marry again in the Bahamas, Royal Bahamian, on December 4th, 2019. We had an amazing time and professional photos that came out nice. During the ceremony, Cheems and I both teared up as we looked into each other's eyes. I felt like I was in a movie, but I wasn't acting. It was a deep moment of peace and complete love.

Our weekends are almost always booked out with dinners, family gatherings, or a full day of binge-watching our favorite shows that are prerecorded so we don't have to deal with commercials. Being social again was a bit tough for me as I had secluded myself from public places for many years. I didn't feel comfortable anymore around crowds and many times became full of anxiety, but in time, Cheems made me feel safe enough and confident enough to get over it all and live in the future.

I can remember the time when I stopped listening to music altogether until he came along. The first time we hung out, I put on that old Adel song. Cheems asked why I would listen to such a depressing song and put on some Motown. I realized then that he was right. Everything I listened to was so negative and depressing. No wonder I was stuck in a funk for so long. I thought it was funny when he asked if I knew any of the music he liked, beings that I knew just about every song out there.

Cheems and I do so much together, more than I ever thought possible. We enjoy fishing, vacations, the shooting range, shooting pool, dancing, entertaining, and sitting in a two-person jacuzzi or hot tub with champagne and music. Every night after he comes home from work, we put the music on and start cooking together while we discuss the day and how it went. We decided, for health reasons, to discontinue meat and dairy from our meals. It's been 4 years now, and we are still going strong. A lot of our friends had a hard time dealing with this, as I suppose there's that fear of the unknown. A lot of them, to this day, still tease us, asking if they should bring a bag of grass for us or something silly like that.

People worry that we don't eat enough or we're not getting enough nutrition, but together we just blow it all off. We do not consider ourselves Vegan, and we don't use labels. We just like our lifestyle and support each other. The meals we make most nights are beautiful and creative. I love that we can do that together. Honestly, I don't know many couples who are lucky enough to have such support.

Again, I'm blessed and grateful.

When all is said and done, I am the first one to admit that I never thought I would meet someone so perfect. I can't imagine ever going back into that old pit of a life I lived, and I can't imagine ever being without this man. I have learned so much from him. How to be patient, kind, empathetic, and focused. He gives me and everyone else the best advice and is always there for anyone, no matter what. He is loyal to us all and would do anything for our kids and pretty much anyone else, for that matter. I look forward to our future together. I look forward to our next vacation and the time we have together. I am truly blessed.

CHAPTER 19 | DNA TEST – WHO AM I? MOVING FORWARD FROM THE PAST

The voices in my head started coming back and repeatedly said, "Kill yourself Suzanne." You are nothing, you have no one, everyone in your family has abandoned you, and you just keep fucking up. You are a loser!" It's funny because these are all of the things my ex-husband said to me repeatedly. I guess I had memorized it all. I also had been suicidal most of my teenage life, and forward, so I was seriously used to abusing myself verbally and physically. The subconscious mind is a mother fucker for sure! Believe me, I do not pretend to have all the answers. I mean, I had gut feelings and transcendental experiences from childhood that stopped me in my tracks, but I couldn't make sense of it all. I would leave my body unwillingly. I would see spirits and dead people a lot, weird synchronicities, and a lot of times, I knew things before they happened.

In 2016 I left my body and saw my real father, a brother who had passed, a newborn baby all the way in the back room, and my grandmother. I lay in my bed as the entry of paralyzation began, knowing that this was it. I'm getting ready to travel now. I lifted out of my body and floated about twelve inches above the floor into the living room, where I saw a man and a younger man both sitting on the couch reading a newspaper, but I couldn't see their faces. The room was lit with orange and yellow light bulbs, and it was foggy. It was like a black-and-white movie but with pale colors. There was an old TV in the background, two small dogs, and one cat. I looked to the other side and saw this beautiful woman with black curly hair wearing a dress and pale blue apron as she was ironing clothes. She turned her head to me, and with her flat burgundy lipstick, she smiled and spoke telepathically.

She said her name was Betty and started pointing to the others, giving their names. I quickly reminded myself not to forget these names, as when you have an out-of-body experience, you are fully aware, and you have full control of yourself when you get good at it. Betty told me their names telepathically, but I had no idea who they were. The details were amazing. Hell, I'm still amazed. You can't make this shit up, and the experiences are so over the top it becomes embossed in your brain. When all was said and done, I quickly called my Aunt TC to see if she knew these names, and she did, but they were the names of other family members. At the time, I knew nothing about my real family, so I chalked it off and thought I had a visitation from my aunts and uncles, that I had never met.

But later, when I took a DNA test and met my family, I found out that they were indeed my father and my grandmother and brother I had never met. The pictures of my father and grandmother that I found on the internet are the same exact faces I saw in my out-of-body experience. This is crazy, but it's also amazing and calming for me to know that they tried to contact me the only way they could.

I chose to take a DNA test to prove to my now husband that I was not Italian. My wonderful husband is 99.99999 % Italian, speaks Italian fluently and is proud. His family immigrated here from Italy as teenagers. They're "off the boat," as the Italians like to say. Since his Italian mother was a redhead, and I am a redhead with a father who had an Italian last name, he swore I was Italian. I tried to explain that women die their hair all the time, but he wasn't having any of that. I think he just wanted me to be Italian. :)

Anyway, I found out I really wasn't Italian. In fact, I have zero Italian in me. Something my mother repeatedly told us growing up, even though we had an Italian last name. That always stuck in my mind. I never understood why she said that so much, and I couldn't understand why everyone around us acted like they were Italian, loved the idea of being Italian, and even inked up their bodies with the boot of Italy. The funny thing is I always knew something wasn't quite right deep down. I mean, other than the simple fact that I am a redhead with white skin and freckles, the obvious, I just knew it. I'd been lied to about my real father and my identity for 53 years, and WOW, that's just awesome!

I vaguely remember my uncle, my mother's younger brother teasing me when I was about nineteen that my mom was with this redhead named Dave and pregnant before she started dating my dad and that Dave was my real father. I thought he was being an idiot because he was sometimes brutally idiotic and told him so. He didn't push that, but when I asked my mother, her response was that he was an asshole. Nothing further, so I just let it go.

After I received my DNA results, I suppose I went into a fog. I looked at it and just walked away. I don't know what happened to me. Maybe my subconscious was trying to protect me? I really don't know. But I ignored it until I started getting emails from two different women asking me if I knew Dave Hatfield or this one or that one. I had no idea what they were talking about. I wasn't doing my family tree, as I gifted that to my aunt, but the emails kept coming. One day after a long period of time not speaking to my mother, I called her and asked if she knew these people. I couldn't understand what her problem was. Why was she getting upset with me? She wound up changing the subject and got mad at me for not bringing the kids around to see her.

This made no sense to me as she had never called my kids even after giving her their cell numbers numerous times, which I reminded her about. Also, the fact that my kids were over eighteen at the time, and the fact that I could barely get a hold of them myself. I mean, did she not remember that I didn't even have the luxury of speaking with them whenever I wanted? She clammed up, then told me that I was upsetting her, and she hung up. I felt like I was in a bad movie or something. WTF was she talking about?! I really didn't even care as I had no warmth in my heart anymore for her. So, after avoiding a call to one of the women for a bit because I felt anxious about it, I finally emailed her my mother's response. I really had no idea why she was so adamant about contacting me, and it was a little stressful, to be honest. Then came the final email that read something like this.

Hi, my name is Tina, and we are a match. I know you don't want to talk to us, but I believe that we are your sisters. If you want to talk, here is my number. The blood quickly drained from my brain down to my toes. WHAT?!! I didn't know what the hell she was talking about. I wasn't avoiding anyone. I just wasn't involved in my family tree. My aunt was. And I had no idea who these people were.

I told my husband, and he stood by me while I made the life-changing call. "We are sisters from the same father." BOOM! Our father is David Hatfield, BOOM! After further conversation, some old pictures of different family members, some who were professional vocalists, a bunch of redheads, the time frame, the conversation with my Uncle, my mom losing her shit over something that made no sense to me, remembering all of the years I had asked her why she picked such an angry man who hates kids to be my father, the fact that I was the only singer in the family, the fact that I was the only redhead in the family and the fact that most of my family on my Dad's side treated me like shit growing up, hit me like a title wave and I dropped to my knees.

At first, I was happy, and within minutes I was devastated because my whole life was a fucking lie. Everyone in my family knew this, but only one, my crazy uncle, had the balls to tell me, but I didn't believe him. Of course, I had heard many stories of other people finding out this type of information later on in life, but I would never in a million years believe that my own mother would do something like this. Hold on to such a major lie for the rest of her days. I was so mad, yet I was so happy at the same time.

I paced for hours until I mustered up the balls to call my father, who I hadn't spoken to in many years. "Hey, Dad, I just wanted to let you know that I took a DNA test and found out that I'm not your daughter." His response: "You're not my daughter, and I'm not your dad. Oh well, have a good life." CLICK! Yep, that was it. The phone rang about two minutes later, and he said, "Hey, I was thinking you owe me some money." I'm embarrassed to say it, but I told him to go F himself and hung up. Never heard from him again. I was so stressed out for hours just thinking about all of this over and over. The lies, the trauma, the betrayal, my brothers. Are they even really my brothers?

I sent my mom a letter since I wasn't ready to stomach her voice or her arrogance. I was upset, of course, but wrote that I forgave her. I just wanted to know about my father, what he was like, and what happened. Like, why did you choose to pretend someone else was my father all of these years?

Jesus! I would have been ecstatic had you told me when I was younger. I'm sure my life and my insecurities, and my relationships would have been completely different. Maybe my real father would have wanted to get to know me. Why did you make me believe the people that hated me were my family for so many years? Everyone knew the truth or had a clue but me. They all lied and kept that dirty secret. She never responded or reached out to me. All I got were crickets... One of my family members said she knew, but it wasn't her business to tell me. I don't look at any of them the same.

God knows I get that people make mistakes, and maybe they thought at the time they were doing the right thing, but why not think ahead a little bit? Think about how your decisions will affect others down the road. Ahh, again they are all unconscious, living in a subconscious program. Alarming! In the end, none of this really matters. I get it. And three years later, I do have empathy for all of them, and I don't care anymore. And I do think it's kinda cool to be connected to a piece of history. The Hatfields and McCoys.

One of my sisters organized a family get-together, and we all met. Now I have 9 or 12 additional siblings. I'm still not really sure about that. But I'm happy that they are all very loving and kind humans.

My new family (Hatfield's)

(Sisters) Tina, Debbie, and Me

My real dad was a redhead like me. David Hatfield. Unfortunately, he passed in 2012, so I won't get to know him in this lifetime.

Dave Hatfield, Dad

That was really upsetting news, and I still wonder how great that would have been to have him there to watch me compete, but I feel him with me here and there. I think the worst part is that no one can tell me anything about him. All I have is two crappy pictures of him and my grandmother in black and white that I found on the internet.

The resemblance is uncanny and gave me some semblance of peace. It took some time, and in so many ways, I am simply relieved. The funny thing is how much my son Bamm resembles my real father. I guess that's why Roman was so confused.

Below is what I received from my DNA test. I'm pretty sure I'm not Italian!

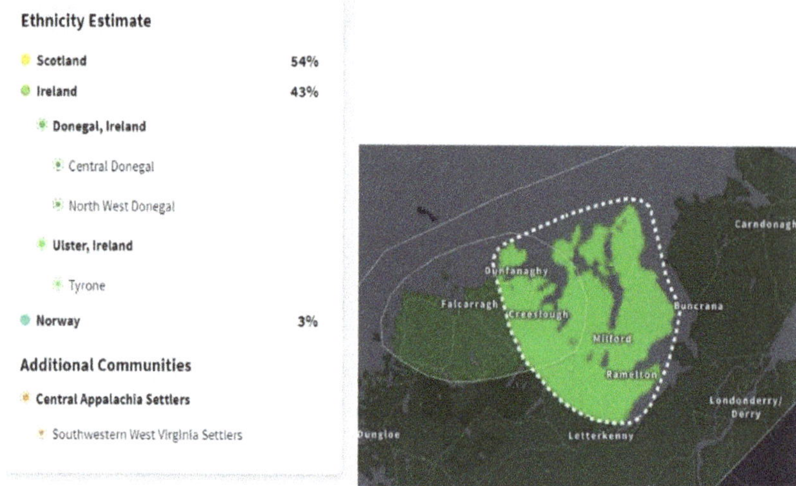

When all was said and done, with my kids, my new family and Cheems family, I literally went from having no one to gaining about thirty or more new family members.

The Chima Family

Mammy, Snuggs, Me & Bamm

There was nothing about Christianity, Catholicism, or any religion for that matter that made any sense to me, especially the idea of a God in the sky that had a long white beard, but I did believe in a higher power. For me, the fact that I have traveled outside of my physical body since I can remember from the age of thirteen, is a showstopper. I joined a group for metaphysical teachings so that I could develop my psychic and energy skills.

I felt like I was locked up in a box and really needed to GTFO ASAP, or I was going to burst.

Part of the lesson was to sit with a stranger, focus, and see if any of the visuals or thoughts that came to me would apply to her. *A psychic reading.* I was not a psychic reader. It took me about a minute to have a vision of a little girl with long hair on a very big horse named Nutmeg riding in a field of beautiful flowers where there were two stables and another horse. There was an elderly Native American lady with braided salt and pepper hair saying "It's gonna be fine. Just be careful."

I have to be honest. I felt like an idiot telling this woman anything, as it made absolutely zero sense to me. And the look on this lady's face was a dead stare. Then she told me that the Native American Woman was her grandmother, who always wore her hair braided. They had a big farm with two horses and stables, and her grandmother would worry because she always rode the biggest horse. That week she was deciding on the name "Nutmeg" for the horse she was going to get in a month.

I guess we cleared that one up. WOW! I have a good friend Lisa that is one of the best psychics I've ever been around. I don't do what she does, at least not on purpose. But the fact that I could sit with a complete stranger and tell them things that made no sense to me but all the sense in the world to them, well, it piqued my interest for sure!

Moving on…

Again and again, I would get these feelings that made me think, this is a joke. Life is such bullshit, it's a fucking game, and the only way to get through it is to win. I had such a bad attitude and encased myself in a full suit of armor 24-7. I couldn't have girlfriends because I didn't trust women, and I never had a normal relationship with a man because I never trusted any man, especially my own father.

"Quick note to remind men that if they have little girls, you will be the first man she falls in love with, so make sure to take care of her well because she will seek out men just like her Daddy to fall in love with."

So, with all of this, as my mind was constantly wandering and vomiting thousands of thoughts profusely, I would randomly try having "the game of life discussions" with friends just to see if I was on the money or close. I guess I wanted validation, but the responses never changed. I was nuts. Eventually, I would talk myself out of my own awareness and continue repeating that old unconscious program over and over again. Because in all reality, it's much easier for most people, to follow the crowd than to be the leader. You would think that I would have done something different, maybe after the first five or ten years of mistakes and not trusting my gut, but I didn't. I waited until I was forty-five to wake up.

I guess I wasn't ready, and even though I sometimes wish that I had woken up sooner, I don't regret my experiences anymore; I understand now that they made me very wise. I understand that I am here for personal expansion and to aid in the expansion of the Universe. And that, to me, is the coolest idea, as woowoo as it may sound.

CHAPTER 21 | MESSAGE TO YOU

My message to you is that I've been down more than once, many, many times. I get it, I lived it, and I got through it despite all the obstacles in my way. And believe me; this story is nowhere close to the worst of my many journeys. But I've figured out a way to feel safe, happy, and incredibly prosperous. I have everything I want and need, and the rest just keeps coming to me. It's miraculous, really. My children get to see me now anytime they want, and they are healing. They are all beautiful human beings with beautiful souls. And I don't feel the need for revenge or to stay angry with anyone who hurt me anymore.

I mean, I did for a while, but now I just stand back and hand that over to the Universe.

I am at peace with everything now, and you can be too. We all can. It just takes a little effort and time. And don't you think you're worth it now?

My beautiful daughter Mammy left the hell hole that she was trapped in many years ago and came to stay with my husband and me. I will totally admit that when her father finally gave up on her and called me to come to get her, it was one of the greatest days ever. Of course, I would have hit the jackpot if my boys had done the same, but they were in a different place emotionally. My Mammy never gave up on me, and she always knew that everything The Parents told her were lies. She has helped me in so many ways to not only understand her better but to understand myself better as well. She has been a great teacher to me without knowing, and as she grows to be a stunning young woman, we continue to get closer and have an unbreakable bond.

 Something I never had with my mother and the way I always wished it was. The funny thing is that she is almost exactly like me in so many ways, so yes, we sometimes butt heads, but she is so much further ahead of this game than I ever was. I now talk to and see all my children frequently. They are much older and have their own lives, but they are voluntarily a part of my life, and that's progress. And despite everything that they have been through, they still somehow managed to be great human beings.

It's amazing to me how many layers I needed to peel away in order to have such a wonderful existence. Changing my mindset, and my actions, diving deep into my childhood self, working through all my trauma, and even writing this book was a major breakthrough for me.

I literally had to relive more than a lot of my traumatic, childhood and adult experiences and work them all out. ***But I couldn't possibly write all my experiences here, so I'll save them for the next book.*** Some days after writing, I would be left in the fetal position, not having the strength to move or function. I had many meltdowns and sleepless nights reliving my traumas through my dreams, only to wake up physically sick and mentally fried. They call this The Dark Night of The Soul and it's wicked! And there were many days when I convinced myself that this was a total waste of time.

The voice inside my head told me that this book would suck, and no one would even read it, let alone learn there is hope. But my practice every day pushed me through. I actually believe that this could have taken me three months to write if I didn't feel so beat down and let it all get to me when I started. I would get glimpses of hope and remember that I am not my thoughts. My thoughts are attached to emotions that are attached to memories, and I can change all of this.

I hope that you enjoyed my story and that it was an easy read. I hope that you have gotten something out of this and that I somehow served you or inspired you. I hope you know that you are loved and that nothing is impossible. There are not many people out there that desire to change because they fear the unknown and they are comfortable with where they are even though they say that they hate their life, but as Dr.Joe Dispenza says, (paraphrasing here) "Why wait to change when you can create your future now?"

Most everything we know was a program from our loving parents, The Parents, and our environment for at least the first seven to thirty years. Wouldn't you feel better if you had control of your own program? Wouldn't you feel better about this life if you knew that you really could have it all and program yourself with the information that best serves you? Are we here to simply meander through each day, waking up, going through our routine, waiting for the day to end just to rinse and repeat? Or are we here to experience the greatness that the Universe has in store for us?

What would your life be like if you simply followed your dreams despite what anyone else has to say about them? There are so many things I want to do now, things I've wanted to do my whole life, but I let the fear of the unknown or someone else's opinion stop me. Now nothing can get in my way because I know that this is my life to live, my joy, my experiences, and I know that nothing is unreachable or unattainable for me or for any of us. There's this influencer named Gary Vee I like to listen to. One of his favorite things he says is, "Fuck what other people think!" He's a little harsh to some, but to me, he's nailed one of the secrets to life and happiness. Fuck what other people think. Who cares. Do you!

Not many will actually take the time to understand where their emotions are coming from and how they affect every move they make. I hope one day to meet you at my seminars and lectures on self-love and mind mastery. But in the meantime, you can start with the teachers I've listed in Chapter 17. Some may not resonate, and that's ok. There were plenty of others that I tried to understand, but there wasn't that flow, so I moved on to the ones that felt right.

Know that we are all a work in progress as long as we are making progress.

Every experience you have, good or bad and even ugly, is a lesson and expansion, and you can choose how you want to feel and how you want to handle them. Remember, it's your show!

As I started doing all these wonderful practices, my life changed drastically.

- **Practicing Self-love:**

(This is a daily must-do!)

- **Meditation:**

(Start with 15 minutes a day and work your way up if you want)

- **Journaling:**

(After every meditation, unload your fears, troubles, and lessons in that book!)

- **Gratitude:**

(Practice until it becomes a habit. Journal what you are grateful for even if you don't have it yet. Write it down as if you do now.)

- **Shadow work:**

(Peel back the layers of trauma, break it all down, forgive yourself, and love your inner child and all your personalities.)

- **Energy work:**

(Even 5 minutes a day before or after your meditation or go outside in nature to ground yourself.)

- **Studying the Laws of Attraction and implementing them:**

(Fascinating stuff, especially when you start to manifest daily)

- **Work out a few days a week:**

(Move your body, you'll thank me when you're older)

- **Eliminate eating animals and dairy if you can.**

(I do eat fish occasionally, eggs, and juice fast here and there. I'm one of not so many at 55 who is not medicated)

- **Turn off the news, and turn off shows that are negative, violent, or pornographic:**

(It doesn't serve any of us, we were good before it all started and better without any of it)

- **Practice consciousness every chance you can:**

(Be aware of your words, your thought patterns, and how you treat others. Be aware of how you feel. And if it's not good, change that!)

- **Practice loving the people who you don't think deserve it:**

(Everyone has their own challenges and personal journey, and you never know what's going on behind closed doors. No one knows what anyone is truly going through, so be kind.)

What is my sole purpose here? I want you to enjoy this book and become empowered by it. I want everyone to know that anything is possible, but you do have to do some work to get there. How much work do you ask?

Well, how fucked up are you? I'm pretty sure you know the answer to that one. It doesn't matter what color you are, what gender, how old you are, or your religion. The Parents probably and unknowingly fucked you up. Their parents fucked them up and so on, going back in time and so forth, moving forward.

In no way do I blame my parents now, nor am I mad anymore because I get it. They were brainwashed and conditioned too, they didn't know any better, and they were afraid of change because it felt uncomfortable and unfamiliar. I don't mean to sound harsh when using the term "brainwashed," it's the only word I find that fits right now.

But I do believe that we all have that voice inside us that is desperately trying to wake us up. It wants us to remember who we truly are. And sometimes it even screams at us, but we have these blinders on. It's all smoke and mirrors, an illusion. We can't see what is right in front of us, and if we do, we doubt ourselves mostly because we're so worried about how others will see us. And trust me, most will think you're nuts, but that's none of your business. It doesn't necessarily need to get deep. It's a simple science and a desire to want more, knowing you deserve to be happy and satisfied in this life. We are all programmed!

I'll take a stab and say you are most likely and pretty much a walking clone of your parents, whether you like it or not.

Unless you take the time to understand how the subconscious works, consciously work on all your different emotions and personalities and become really clear on who you purposefully want to be, you're on a program, and it probably blows! I don't care how much you pray; God/The Universe doesn't give to those who are not ready to receive. And to receive is to feel as if you already have what you want, to love, to have grace, and to be happy. You cannot receive what you want if you are pondering what you don't have.

I promise you no matter what age, no matter what, you can have anything you want if you really want it, but only if you're willing to do the work. I've wanted to write this book since I was sixteen years old, and when it's finished this year, 2023, it will be forty years in the waiting. Forty years of wanting to do something but having every excuse you could possibly imagine and putting it off. What if it sucks? What if no one likes it?

What if I sound dumb? What if I fail? OMG, I'm literally showing everyone how messed up and dumb I was.

Yadda, yadda, yadda. Brain trash was seeping through my eyes. When all the time, I just needed to be in the right mindset to be able to heal while I was going back in time and regurgitating/re-living all of this bullshit. That was a whole show, indeed, and I survived.

At this point in my life, I practice morning meditations and mindfulness every day. If I missed a meditation, my day was shit. I'd actually feel guilty about that for a minute but remembered to accept that I'll never stop learning on this journey and that my inner source loves me no matter what and eventually find an hour or twenty minutes to meditate and reconnect.

I know that I came here with a purpose. Not to be pretty or smart or wealthy, although these are fun things. I came here to learn how to experience the best in life. To find my uniqueness, and my passions, to have fun, play, and laugh. To smile and *trust me, that was hard!* To rendezvous with other humans and experience contrast, learn lessons, and expand. I want to teach others that are still stuck and who have been in similar, abusive situations how to break free from the chains that have been holding them back and holding them down.

Many of us continually ask, "What is my purpose here?" And for a lot of us, this is the hardest question we will ever need an answer to. From the time I was three, I have been singing. By the time I was nine, I knew I wanted to be a rockstar. I wanted to perform in front of millions of people all over the world. And on the down low, I still do, but I'm older now, and after losing my voice for so long, I kinda gave up on those details and just sing in my basement with my husband. But I know that I will use my voice for bigger things, like this book, for a start.

So now what will I do with my life? I will do everything I dream of no matter how hard or how challenging it may be. I will love myself first unconditionally, and I will do my best to stay conscious, not judge, and have more compassion for everyone I encounter on my journey.

Having my own business sounds great, but it would have to be something I'm passionate about. What am I good at was the real question. Well, I have experienced a ton of trauma and survived it. I learned, and I'm still learning every day, how to rewire my mind and retrain my body. I can certainly help other people who have been through similar experiences as long as they are willing to do the work.

I realized that I am powerfully positioned from my experiences to serve the person I once was. We all are. Once you get that and really let it sink in, you will find your purpose. Maybe that's what we are all here for.

In the meantime, live, laugh, and love everything around you because life is too short to waste it on other people's opinions and judgments. Take risks, challenge yourself, and be persistent on your journey to be the best you can be. Be a leader, and lead by example because words don't teach. Do you, be you, embrace your self-worth, and love yourself because, in the end, you and your inner being are all that you have.

I just want you to remember that average is the enemy, success is your responsibility, and change can take place in an instant if you are willing and ready to flip the switch.

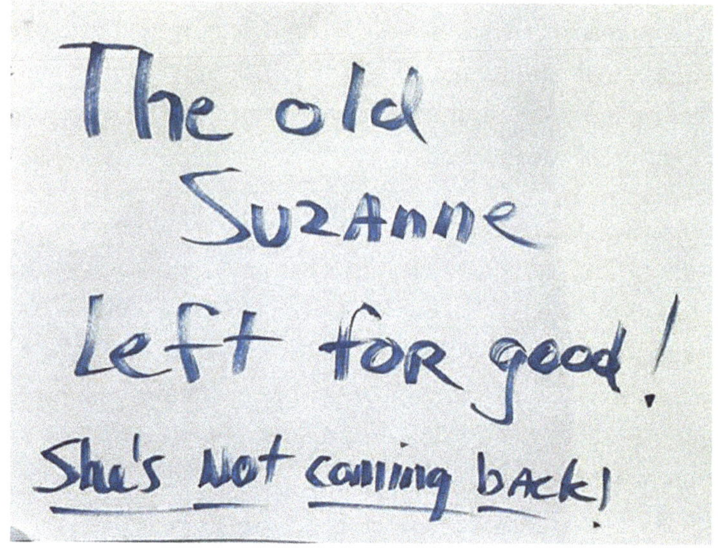